Guitar Chord Songbook

Praise &
Worship

ISBN-13: 978-0-634-07338-0
ISBN-10: 0-634-07338-9

HAL•LEONARD®
CORPORATION

7777 W. BLUEMOUND RD. P.O. BOX 13819 MILWAUKEE, WI 53213

Visit Hal Leonard Online at
www.halleonard.com

Guitar Chord Songbook

Contents

4 Above All

6 Agnus Dei

10 All Things Are Possible

12 Ancient of Days

14 As the Deer

7 Awesome God

16 Be Glorified

18 Be Unto Your Name

20 Better Is One Day

22 Breathe

19 Celebrate Jesus

24 Change My Heart Oh God

25 Come, Now Is the Time to Worship

26 Create in Me a Clean Heart

28 Cry of My Heart

30 Days of Elijah

32 Did You Feel the Mountains Tremble?

27 Draw Me Close

34 Enough

36 Every Move I Make

38 Everyday

40 Firm Foundation

42 Forever

43 Give Thanks

44 Glorify Thy Name

46 God Is Good All the Time

48 God of Wonders

50 Great Is the Lord

52 Hallelujah (Your Love Is Amazing)

54 He Has Made Me Glad

53 He Is Exalted

56 The Heart of Worship

58 Here I Am to Worship

60 Holiness

62 Holy and Anointed One

64 How Majestic Is Your Name

66 Hungry (Falling on My Knees)

68 I Could Sing of Your Love Forever

67 I Give You My Heart

70 I Love to Be In Your Presence

71 I Love You Lord

72 I Stand in Awe

74 I Want to Know You

73 I Will Exalt Your Name

76 It Is You

78 Jesus, Lover of My Soul

80 Jesus, Name Above All Names

82 Knowing You (All I Once Held Dear)

84 Lamb of God

86 Let Everything That Has Breath

88 Light the Fire Again

90 Lord, Reign in Me

92 Lord, I Lift Your Name on High

81 More Love, More Power

94 More Precious than Silver

95 My God Reigns

96 My Life Is in You, Lord

97 My Redeemer Lives

98 Oh Lord, You're Beautiful

102 Open the Eyes of My Heart

104 The Potter's Hand

101 Refiner's Fire

106 Sanctuary

110 Shine, Jesus, Shine

107 Shine on Us

112 Shout to the Lord

114 Shout to the North

116 So Good to Me

118 Step by Step

120 There Is a Redeemer

122 This Is the Day

124 Trading My Sorrows

126 We Bow Down

123 We Fall Down

128 We Want to See Jesus Lifted High

130 We Will Glorify

132 Worthy, You Are Worthy

136 You Alone

138 You Are My King (Amazing Love)

133 You Are So Good to Me

Above All

Words and Music by
Paul Baloche and Lenny LeBlanc

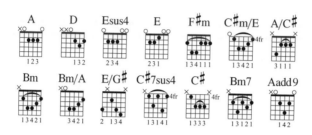

Intro

| A | D | Esus4 E | A | D | A | |

Verse 1

| | D | Esus4 | A |
Above all powers,   above all kings,

| | D | E | A |
Above all nature and all ___ created things;

| | F#m | C#m/E | D | A/C# |
Above all wisdom and all ___ the ways of man,

Bm   **Bm/A**   **E/G#**   **A**
You were here before ___ the world began.

Verse 2

A/C#   **D**   **Esus4**   **A**
A-bove all kingdoms,   above all thrones,

A/C#   **D**   **E**   **A**
A-bove all wonders the world ___ has ever known;

       F#m   **C#m/E**   **D**   **A/C#**
Above all wealth and treas - ures of the earth,

Bm   **D**   **C#7sus4**   **C#**
There's no way to meas - ure what You're worth.

Chorus 1

```
A          Bm7   E/G♯        A
Crucified, _____ laid behind a stone,
                 Bm7  E/G♯        A
You lived to die ___ re - jected and alone.
E/G♯        F♯m  C♯m/E           D  A/C♯
Like a rose _____ trampled on the ground,
                 Bm7  A/C♯
You took the fall
                 D  E      A
And thought of me ___   above all.
```

Interlude 1 | D   Esus4 E | A   D   A |

Verse 3   *Repeat Verse 1*

Verse 4   *Repeat Verse 2*

Chorus 2

```
A          Bm7   E/G♯        A
Crucified, _____ laid behind a stone,
                 Bm7  E/G♯        A
You lived to die ___ re - jected and alone.
E/G♯        F♯m  C♯m/E           D  A/C♯
Like a rose _____ trampled on the ground,
                 Bm7  A/C♯
You took the fall
                 D  E      A   Bm7   E/G♯
And thought of me ___   above all.
```

Chorus 3   *Repeat Chorus 1*

Outro

```
E/G♯        F♯m  C♯m/E           D  A/C♯
Like a rose _____ trampled on the ground,
                 Bm7  A/C♯
You took the fall
                 D  E      A
And thought of me ___   above all.
| D    Esus4 E | Aadd9        ‖
```

Agnus Dei

Words and Music by
Michael W. Smith

Melody:

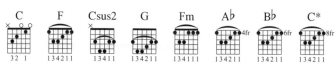

Al - le - lu - ia, _____

C   F   Csus2   G   Fm   A♭   B♭   C*

Intro   ‖: C | :‖ *Play 4 times*
                   | F | | | |

Verse 1   C   F C   F   C
               Alle - lu - ia, alle-luia, for our Lord God Almighty ___ reigns.

               C   F C   F   C   F
               Alle - lu - ia, alle-luia, for our Lord God Almighty ___ reigns. Alle-luia.

Chorus 1   Csus2
               Ho-ly, holy are You, Lord God Almighty.

                           F
               Worthy is the Lamb, worthy is the Lamb.

                     Csus2   G
               You are ho - ly, holy are You, Lord God Almight - y.

                           F   Csus2
               Worthy is the Lamb, worthy is the Lamb. You are ho - ly.

Verse 2   *Repeat Verse 1*

Chorus 2   Csus2
               Ho-ly, holy are You, Lord God Almighty.

                           F
               Worthy is the Lamb, worthy is the Lamb.

                     Csus2   G
               You are ho - ly, holy are You, Lord God Almight - y.

                           F   Fm   C
               Worthy is the Lamb, worthy is the Lamb. You are ho - ly.

                     A♭ B♭   C*
Outro   ‖:   You are ho - ly.   :‖ *Repeat and fade*

Awesome God

Melody:

Words and Music by
Rich Mullins

When He rolls up His sleeve, He ain't just "put-tin' on the Ritz."

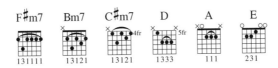

| F#m7 | Bm7 | C#m7 | D | A | E |
| 131111 | 13121 | 13121 | 1333 | 111 | 231 |

Intro | F#m7 | Bm7 C#m7 | F#m7 | Bm7 C#m7 |

Verse 1
            F#m
When He rolls up His sleeve, He ain't just "puttin' on the Ritz."
   Bm7   C#m7   F#m
Our God is an awesome God!

There is thunder in His footsteps and lightnin' in His fist.
   Bm7   C#m7   F#m
Our God is an awesome God!

     Bm7
And the Lord wasn't jokin' when He kicked 'em out of Eden;
   C#m7
It wasn't for no reason that He shed His blood.
      D   Bm7
His re-turn is very close and so you better be believin' that our
     C#m7   F#m
God is an awesome God!

Chorus 1

     D   **A**
Our God is an awesome God;

     E   **F♯m**
He reigns from heaven above.

     D   **A**
With wisdom, pow'r and love,

    Bm7   **C♯m7**   **F♯m**
Our God is an awesome God!

     D   **A**
Our God is an awesome God;

     E   **F♯m**
He reigns from heaven above.

     D   **A**
With wisdom, pow'r and love,

    Bm7   **C♯m7**   **F♯m**
Our God is an awesome God!

| **Bm7** **C♯m7** |

Verse 2

           F♯m
And when the sky was starless in the void of the night,

    Bm7   **C♯m7**   **F♯m**
Our God is an awesome God!

He spoke into the darkness and created the light.

    Bm7   **C♯m7** **F♯m**
Our God is an awesome God!

    Bm7
The judgment and wrath He poured out on Sodom,

    C♯m7
The mercy and grace He gave us at the cross.

    D   **Bm7**
I hope that we have not too quickly forgotten

        C♯m7   **F♯m**
That our God is an awesome God!

Chorus 2   _Repeat Chorus 1_

Chorus 3
          D   **A**
Our God is an awesome God;

        E   **F♯m**
He reigns from heaven above.

          D   **A**
With wisdom, pow'r and love,

        Bm7   **C♯m7**   **F♯m**
Our God is an awesome God!

          D   **A**
Our God is an awesome God;

        E   **F♯m**
He reigns from heaven above.

          D   **A**
With wisdom, pow'r and love,

        Bm7   **C♯m7**   **F♯m**
Our God is an awesome God!

        Bm7   **C♯m7**   **F♯m**
Our God is an awesome God!

        Bm7   **C♯m7**   **F♯m**
Our God is an awesome God!

All Things Are Possible

Words and Music by
Darlene Zschech

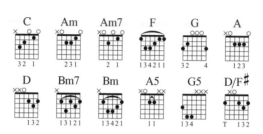

Intro ‖: C | Am | C | Am7 :‖

Verse 1

C   Am7
Almighty God, ___ my Redeemer,

C   Am7
My hiding place, ___ my safe refuge.

F   G
No other name ___ like Jesus,

F   G
No pow'r can stand ___ against You.

Verse 2

C   Am7
My feet are plant - ed on this Rock,

C   Am7
And I will not ___ be shaken.

F   G
My hope, it comes ___ from You alone,

F   G   A
My Lord and my ___ Salva - tion.

Bridge 1

```
        D              Bm7
        Your praise is al - ways on my lips.

        D              Bm7
        Your word is liv - ing in my heart,

        G            A           Bm   A
        And I will praise ____ You with a new  song.

        G            A
        My soul will bless ____ You, Lord.

        D              Bm7
        You will fill my life ____ with greater joy.

        D            Bm7
        Yes, I delight ____ myself in You,

        G            A           Bm   A
        And I will praise ____ You with a new  song.

        G            A
        My soul will bless ____ You, Lord.
```

Interlude 1 | C | Am | C | Am7 |

Verse 3   *Repeat Verse 2*

Bridge 2   *Repeat Bridge 1*

Chorus 1

```
              Bm       A5      G5
        When I am weak You make me strong.

        D/F♯      G    Bm      A5         Bm   A5   G5
        When I'm poor I know I'm rich, for in the power of Your name

        A5  N.C.              G5  A5  N.C.                G5
           All things are possible,      all things are possible,

        A5  N.C.                 G5  A5  N.C.            A
           All things are possible,      all things are pos - sible.
```

Bridge 3   *Repeat Bridge 1*

Chorus 2

```
              Bm       A5      G5
        When I am weak You make me strong.

        D/F♯      G    Bm      A5         Bm   A5   G5
        When I'm poor I know I'm rich, for in the power of Your name

           A5  N.C.              G5  A5  N.C.
      ‖:     All things are possible,      all things are possible,

        G5  A5  N.C.                G5  A5  N.C.
           All things are possible,         all things are possible.  :‖

        G5  A5  N.C.              A5
           All things are possible.
```

Ancient of Days

Words and Music by
Gary Sadler and Jamie Harvill

Bless-ing __ and hon - or,   glo - ry __ and pow - er

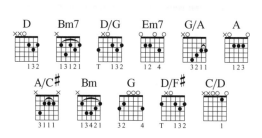

Intro | D | Bm7 | D/G | Em7 G/A A |

Verse 1
D   A/C♯ Bm A/C♯
Blessing and honor, glory and power be unto the Ancient of Days.

D   Bm7   A/C♯ D
From ev'ry nation, all of creation, bow before the Ancient of Days.

Chorus 1
G   Em7   A   D/F♯
Ev'ry tongue from heaven and earth   shall declare ____ Your glory.

G   Em7   A   D/F♯
Ev'ry knee shall bow at Your throne ____ in worship.

G   Em7   A
You will be ex-alted, O God,

D/F♯ G   Em7   A   G/A   D
And Your kingdom shall not pass away, ____ O Ancient of Days.

Verse 2	*Repeat Verse 1*
Chorus 2	*Repeat Chorus 1*

Bridge

    D
Your kingdom shall reign over all the earth.

C/D   **D**
Sing unto the Ancient of Days.

For none can compare to Your matchless worth.

C/D   **D**
Sing unto the Ancient of Days.

Chorus 3   *Repeat Chorus 1*

Outro

  G/A   **D** **G/A**   **D**
O Ancient of Days, ____ O Ancient of Days.

As the Deer

Words and Music by
Martin Nystrom

Melody:

As the deer pant-eth for the wa-ter, so my

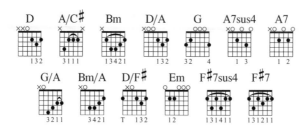

D   A/C#   Bm   D/A   G   A7sus4   A7

G/A   Bm/A   D/F#   Em   F#7sus4   F#7

Intro

|D A/C# |Bm D/A |G A7sus4 |D |

Verse 1

D   A/C#   Bm   D/A
As the deer panteth for the water,

      G   A7sus4 A7   D   G/A A7
So my soul longeth af   -   ter Thee.

D   A/C#   Bm   D/A
You a - lone are my heart's de - sire

      G   A7sus4 A7   D
And I long to wor   -   ship Thee.

Chorus 1

Bm Bm/A   G   D/F#
You a - lone are my strength, my shield;

   G   Bm   Em F#7sus4 F#7
To You a - lone may my spirit yield.

D   A/C#   Bm   D/A
You a - lone are my heart's de - sire

      G   A7sus4 A7   D
And I long to wor   -   ship Thee.

Verse 2

D   A/C♯   Bm   D/A
You're my friend and You are my brother,

     G   A7sus4 A7   D   G/A A7
Even though You are _____ a King.

D   A/C♯   Bm   D/A
I love you more than any oth - er,

      G   A7sus4 A7 D
So much more than any   -   thing.

Chorus 2   *Repeat Chorus 1*

Verse 3

D   A/C♯   Bm   D/A
I want You more than gold or silver,

     G   A7sus4 A7 D G/A A7
Only You can sat   -   is-fy.

D   A/C♯   Bm   D/A
You a - lone are the real joy giver,

     G   A7sus4 A7   D
And the apple of _____ my eye.

Chorus 3   *Repeat Chorus 1*

Outro

D   A/C♯   Bm   D/A
You a - lone are my heart's de - sire

     G   A7sus4 A7   D
And I long to wor   -   ship Thee.

Be Glorified

Words and Music by Louie Giglio,
Chris Tomlin and Jesse Reeves

Melody:

Your love _ has cap - tured _ me, _

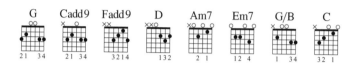

Intro ‖: G   Cadd9 |Fadd9   Cadd9 :‖

Verse 1
G   Cadd9 Fadd9   Cadd9
Your love has captured me,

G   Cadd9   D
Your grace has set me free;

G   Cadd9 Fadd9 Cadd9
Your life, the air I   breathe.

Am7   D   G
Be glorified ____ in me.

Interlude 1   *Repeat Intro*

Chorus 1

Cadd9   G
You set my feet to dancing,   You set my heart on fire.

     Cadd9   G
In the presence of a thousand kings, You are my one desire.

Cadd9
And I stand before You now

    Em7   D   Cadd9   G
With trembling hands lifted high. _____ Be glorified.

Interlude 2   *Repeat Intro*

Verse 2   *Repeat Verse 1*

Chorus 2   *Repeat Chorus 1*

Bridge

    G   G/B   C   D   G/B   C   D
‖: Be glo - ri - fied in me, be glo - ri - fied in me,

       G/B   C   D   G/B   C
Be glo - ri - fied in me, be glo - ri - fied. :‖

Chorus 3   *Repeat Chorus 1*

Outro   ‖: G   Cadd9 | Fadd9   Cadd9 :‖ G   ‖

Be Unto Your Name

Words and Music by
Lynn DeShazo and Gary Sadler

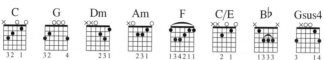

Verse 1

C   G   Dm   Am
We are a mo - ment, You are forev - er,

F   C/E Bb   Gsus4 G
Lord of the ag - es, God before time.

C   G   Dm   Am
We are a va - por, You are eter - nal,

F   C/E Bb   Gsus4 G
Love everlast - ing, reigning on high.

Chorus 1

Am F C/E   G
Holy, holy, Lord God Almight - y.

Am   F   C   Gsus4 G
Worthy is the Lamb who was slain.

Am   F   C/E   G
Highest praises, honor and glo - ry

Dm   Am   Gsus4 G Dm   Am   Gsus4 G
Be un - to Your name, _____ be un - to Your name.

Verse 2

C   G   Dm   Am
We are the bro - ken, You are the heal - er,

F   C/E Bb   Gsus4 G
Jesus, redeem - er, mighty to save.

C   G   Dm   Am
You are the love __ song we'll sing for - ever,

F   C/E Bb   Gsus4 G
Bowing before _ You, blessing Your name.

Chorus 2

Repeat Chorus 1

| C   ‖

Celebrate Jesus

Words and Music by
Gary Oliver

Melody:

Cel - e - brate Je - sus, cel -

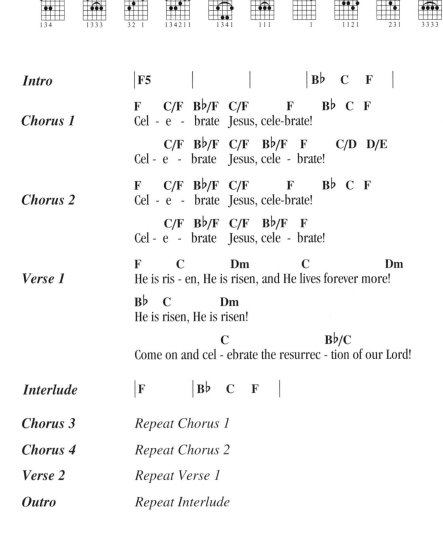

F5   Bb   C   F   C/F   Bb/F   C/D   D/E   Dm   Bb/C

Intro
| F5 | | | | Bb C F |

Chorus 1

F   C/F Bb/F C/F   F   Bb C F
Cel - e - brate Jesus, cele-brate!

       C/F Bb/F C/F Bb/F F   C/D D/E
Cel - e - brate Jesus, cele - brate!

Chorus 2

F   C/F Bb/F C/F   F   Bb C F
Cel - e - brate Jesus, cele-brate!

       C/F Bb/F C/F Bb/F F
Cel - e - brate Jesus, cele - brate!

Verse 1

F   C   Dm   C   Dm
He is ris - en, He is risen, and He lives forever more!

Bb   C   Dm
He is risen, He is risen!

          C   Bb/C
Come on and cel - ebrate the resurrec - tion of our Lord!

Interlude
| F | Bb C F | |

Chorus 3   *Repeat Chorus 1*

Chorus 4   *Repeat Chorus 2*

Verse 2   *Repeat Verse 1*

Outro   *Repeat Interlude*

Better Is One Day

Words and Music by
Matt Redman

Melody:

How love-ly is Your dwell-ing place,

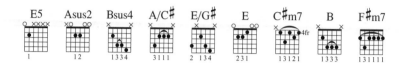

E5   Asus2   Bsus4   A/C#   E/G#   E   C#m7   B   F#m7

Intro

| E5 | | | | |

Verse 1

    E5   Asus2   Bsus4
How lovely is Your dwelling place,   O Lord Almight - y,

    E5   Bsus4
For my soul longs and ever faints for You,

    E5   Asus2   Bsus4
For here my heart is satisfied   within Your pres - ence.

    E5   Bsus4
I sing beneath the shadow of Your wings.

Chorus 1

    Asus2   Bsus4
Better is one day in Your courts, better is one day in Your house,

    Asus2   A/C#   Bsus4
Better is one day in Your courts than thousands elsewhere.

  E/G# Asus2   Bsus4
Better is one day in Your courts, better is one day in Your house,

    Asus2   A/C#   Bsus4
Better is one day in Your courts than thousands elsewhere,

               E   E5
Than thousands elsewhere.

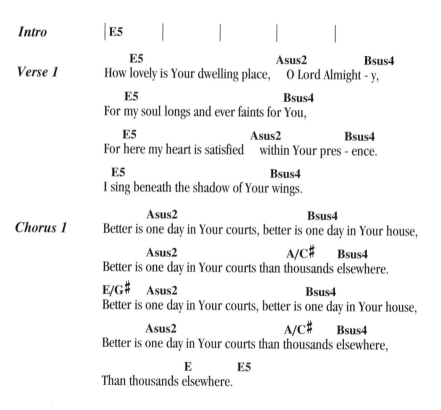

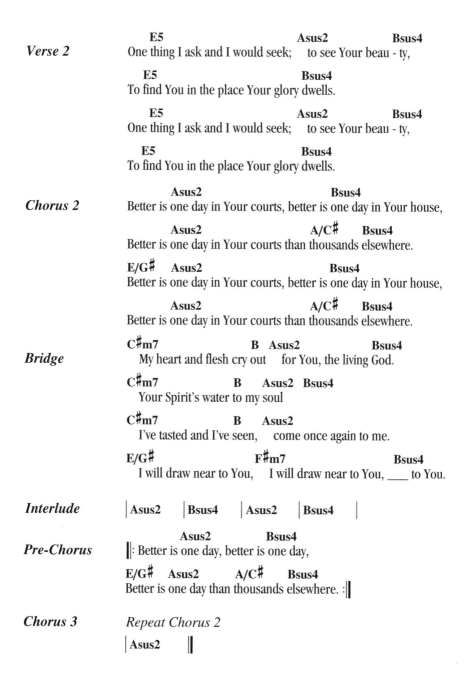

Verse 2

E5   Asus2   Bsus4
One thing I ask and I would seek; to see Your beau - ty,

E5   Bsus4
To find You in the place Your glory dwells.

E5   Asus2   Bsus4
One thing I ask and I would seek; to see Your beau - ty,

E5   Bsus4
To find You in the place Your glory dwells.

Chorus 2

    Asus2   Bsus4
Better is one day in Your courts, better is one day in Your house,

    Asus2   A/C♯ Bsus4
Better is one day in Your courts than thousands elsewhere.

E/G♯ Asus2   Bsus4
Better is one day in Your courts, better is one day in Your house,

    Asus2   A/C♯ Bsus4
Better is one day in Your courts than thousands elsewhere.

Bridge

C♯m7   B Asus2   Bsus4
 My heart and flesh cry out for You, the living God.

C♯m7   B Asus2 Bsus4
 Your Spirit's water to my soul

C♯m7   B Asus2
 I've tasted and I've seen, come once again to me.

E/G♯   F♯m7   Bsus4
 I will draw near to You, I will draw near to You, ___ to You.

Interlude | Asus2 | Bsus4 | Asus2 | Bsus4 |

Pre-Chorus

    Asus2   Bsus4
‖: Better is one day, better is one day,

E/G♯ Asus2   A/C♯ Bsus4
Better is one day than thousands elsewhere. :‖

Chorus 3   *Repeat Chorus 2*

    | Asus2 ‖

Breathe

Words and Music by
Marie Barnett

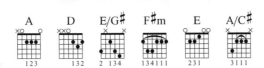

Verse

    A   D   A   D
This is the air ____ I breathe,   this is the air ____ I breathe,

A   E/G♯ F♯m E D   A/C♯ E
Your ho - ly pres - ence   living ____ in me.

    A   D   A   D
This is the air ____ I breathe,   this is the air ____ I breathe,

A   E/G♯ F♯m E D   A/C♯ E
Your ho - ly pres - ence   living ____ in me.

Chorus 1

    A E/G♯ F♯m E   D   F♯m E
And I, _____ I'm desp'rate for You.

      A E/G♯ F♯m E   D   F♯m E
And I, _____ I'm lost without ____ You.

           D A E
Oh, Lord, I'm lost without You,

       D   A   E
I'm lost with-out You, ____ and You are my daily bread.

© 1995 MERCY/VINEYARD PUBLISHING (ASCAP)
Admin. in North America by MUSIC SERVICES o/b/o VINEYARD MUSIC GLOBAL INC.
All Rights Reserved   Used by Permission

Bridge
      A   D   A   D
This is my dai - ly bread,   this is my dai - ly bread,

      A   E/G♯ F♯m E D   F♯m   E
Your ver - y Word   spoken ___ to me.

      A   D   A   D
This is my dai - ly bread,   this is my dai - ly bread,

      A   E/G♯ F♯m E D   F♯m   E
Your ver - y Word   spoken ___ to me.

Chorus 2
        A E/G♯ F♯m E   D   F♯m E
And I, _____   I'm desp'rate for You.

        A E/G♯ F♯m E   D   F♯m E
And I, _____   I'm lost without ___ You.

            D   F♯m E   D   F♯m
I'm lost without ___ You,   I'm nothing with-out You.
|E |D F♯m |E   ‖

Change My Heart Oh God

Words and Music by
Eddie Espinosa

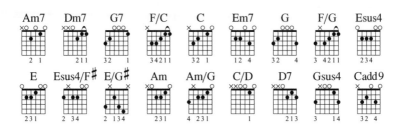

Intro

| Am7 | Dm7 | G7 | F/C | |

Chorus 1

C   Em7   Dm7 G F/G G C
Change my heart, oh God, ____ make it ever ____ true.

Am7   Dm7 G7   C
Change my heart, oh God, ____   may I be like You.

Verse

Esus4 E Esus4/F♯ E/G♯ Am
  You are   the Potter,

Dm7 G7   C
 I am the clay.

Esus4 E Esus4/F♯ E/G♯ Am Am/G
 Mold me   and make me,

C/D   D7 Gsus4 G
This is what I pray.

Chorus 2

C   Em7   Dm7 G F/G G C
Change my heart, oh God, ____ make it ever ____ true.

Am7   Dm7 G7   F/C Cadd9
Change my heart, oh God, ____   may I be like You.

Come, Now Is the Time to Worship

Words and Music by
Brian Doerksen

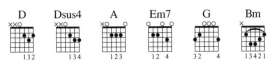

Chorus 1	**D** **Dsus4 D** Come, now is the time to wor - ship.
	A **Em7** **G** Come, now is the time to give your heart.
	D **Dsus4 D** Come, just as you are, to wor - ship.
	A **Em7** **G** **D** Come, just as you are, be-fore your God. Come.
Verse	**G** **D** One day ev'ry tongue will confess ____ You are God.
	G **D** One day ev'ry knee will bow.
	G **Bm** Still, the greatest treasure remains for those
	Em7 **A** Who glad - ly choose You now. ____
Chorus 2	*Repeat Chorus 1*

Create in Me a Clean Heart

Words and Music by
Keith Green

Cre - ate in me a clean heart, ___

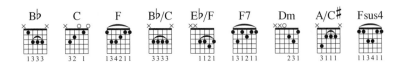

Bb	C	F	Bb/C	Eb/F	F7	Dm	A/C#	Fsus4
1333	32 1	134211	3333	1121	131211	231	3111	113411

Intro | **Bb** | **C** | **F** | **Bb/C C** |

Verse

    C F   **C**   **Bb**   **F**
Cre-ate in me a clean heart, ____ O God,

                C   **F Bb C**
And renew a right spirit within me.

      F   **C**   **Bb**   **F**
Cre-ate in me a clean heart, ____ O God,

            C   **F Eb/F F7**
And renew a right spirit within me.

Bb   **C**   **F**   **C Dm**
Cast me not a-way from Thy presence, O Lord,

    Bb   **C**   **F Eb/F F7**
And take not Thy Holy Spirit from me.

    Bb   **C** **A/C#**   **Dm**
Re-store unto me the joy of Thy sal-vation,

Bb   **C**   **Fsus4 F**
And renew a right spirit within me.

Draw Me Close

Words and Music by
Kelly Carpenter

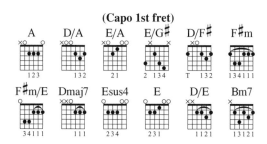

Verse

| A | | D/A E/A | A |
Draw me close to You, never let me go.

E/G♯   D/F♯   F♯m F♯m/E   Dmaj7
I lay it all down ___ again to hear You say that I'm ___ Your friend.

A   D/A E/A   A
You are my desire, no one else will do.

E/G♯   D/F♯
'Cause nothing else could take ___ Your place

F♯m F♯m/E   Dmaj7
To feel the warmth of Your ___ embrace.

A   D/A Esus4   E   A D/E E
Help me find the way, bring me back ___ to You.

Chorus

A   E/A D/A A   E/G♯ D/F♯   Esus4 E
You're all ___ I want, You're all ___ I ev - er need - ed.

A   E/A D/A Bm7   E   A
You're all ___ I want. Help me know You are near.

Cry of My Heart

Words and Music by
Terry Butler

It is the cry of my heart to fol - low You.

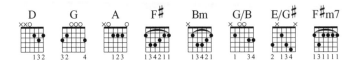

Intro |D G |A F♯ |G A |D G A |

Chorus 1
    D   G   A   G
    It is the cry of my heart   to fol - low You.

    D   G   A   G
    It is the cry of my heart   to be close ____ to You.

    D   G   A F♯
    It is the cry of my heart   to follow

    G   A   D G A
    All of the days ____ of my life.

Chorus 2
    D   G   A   G
    It is the cry of my heart   to fol - low You.

    D   G   A   G
    It is the cry of my heart   to be close ____ to You.

    D   G   A F♯
    It is the cry of my heart   to follow

    G   A   D
    All of the days ____ of my life.

Verse 1

Bm   G/B   A   D
   Teach me Your holy ways, ___ O Lord,

Bm   E/G♯   A
So I can walk ___ in Your truth.

Bm   G/B   A   D
   Teach me Your holy ways, ___ O Lord,

      G   A   D G A
And make me wholly devot - ed to You.

Chorus 3   *Repeat Chorus 2*

Verse 2

Bm G/B A   D
  Open my eyes so I ___ can see

 Bm   E/G♯   A
The wonderful things ___ that You do.

Bm G/B   A   D
  Open my heart up more ___ and more,

      G   A   D G A
And make me wholly devot - ed to You.

Chorus 4

D   G   A   G
  It is the cry of my heart to fol - low You.

D   G   A   G
  It is the cry of my heart to be close ___ to You.

D   G   A F♯
  It is the cry of my heart to follow

G   A   D F♯m7
All of the days ___ of my life.

G   A   D F♯m7
All of the days ___ of my life.

G   A   D
All of the days ___ of my life.

Days of Elijah

Words and Music by
Robin Mark

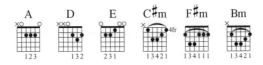

Verse 1

    A   D
These are the days of E - lijah,

      A   E   A
De - claring the Word of the Lord.

                  D
And these are the days of Your servant, Moses

A   E   A
Righteousness being re - stored.

   C#m   F#m
And though these are days of great trials,

   Bm   D   E   N.C.
Of famine and darkness and sword,

     A   D
Still we are the voice in the desert crying,

      A   E   A
"Pre - pare ye the way ____ of the Lord."

Chorus 1

      A   D
Behold, He comes, riding on the clouds,

                A   E
Shining like the sun ____ at the trumpet call.

     A   D
Lift your voice, it's the year of Jubilee

           A   E   A
And out of Zion's hill sal-vation comes.

Interlude 1	|D |A |E |

Verse 2

       A   **D**
And these are the days of E-zekiel,

       A   **E**   **A**
The dry bones be-coming as flesh.

                       D
And these are the days of Your servant, David,

       A   **E**   **A**
Re - building a temple of praise.

     C♯m   **F♯m**
And these are the days of the harvest,

     Bm   **D**   **E**   **N.C.**
The fields are as white in the world.

     A   **D**
And we are the laborers in Your vineyard,

     A   **E**   **A**
De - claring the Word ____ of the Lord.

Chorus 2   *Repeat Chorus 1*

Interlude 2   *Repeat Interlude 1*

Bridge

    A   **D**
||: There is no God like Jehovah,   there is no God like Jehovah,

A
There is no God like Jehovah,

E
There is no God like Jehovah. :|| *Play 4 times*

Did You Feel the Mountains Tremble?

Words and Music by
Martin Smith

Csus2 Am7 Dm7 Fsus2 G7sus4 C Gsus4 F/A G5

Intro | Csus2 | | | |

Verse 1
    Csus2
Did you feel the mountains tremble?

    Am7
  Did you hear the oceans roar

Dm7   **Fsus2**
  When the people rose to sing of   Jesus Christ,

    G7sus4 **C**
The risen   One?

Interlude 1 | Csus2 | Gsus4 | Csus2 | Gsus4 |

Verse 2
    Csus2
  Did you feel the people tremble?

    Am7
  Did you hear the singers roar

Dm7   **Fsus2**
  When the lost began to sing of   Jesus Christ,

    G7sus4 **C**   **Csus2**
The saving   One?

              F/A   **C**
Pre-Chorus 1   And we can see that, God, You're mov - ing

       F/A   **C**
A mighty river through the na - tions;

           F/A   **C**
And young and old will turn to Je - sus.

Chorus 1

Dm7
Fling wide, you heavenly gates;

Fsus2   G7sus4 Csus2 Gsus4 Csus2 Gsus4
Prepare the way of the risen   Lord.

Bridge 1

C   F/A
Open up the doors. Let the music play.

Dm7   C   G5
Let the streets resound with singing.

C   F/A
Songs that bring Your hope, songs that bring Your joy,

Dm7   C   G5
Dancers who dance upon injus-tice.

Verse 3

Csus2
Do you feel the darkness tremble

Am7
When all the saints join in one song,

Dm7
And all the streams flow as one river

Fsus2   G7sus4 C   Csus2
To wash away our broken - ness?

Pre-Chorus 2

              F/A   C
And here we see that, God, You're mov - ing;

         F/A   C
A time of jubilee is com - ing,

             F/A   C
When young and old return to Je - sus.

Chorus 2   *Repeat Chorus 1*

Bridge 2   *Repeat Bridge 1*

| Csus2 ‖

Enough

Words and Music by
Chris Tomlin and Louie Giglio

All of You __ is more than e - nough __

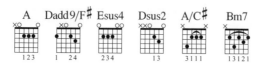

Chorus 1

    A **Dadd9/F♯**   **Esus4** **Dsus2**
All of You is more than enough ___ for

    A   **Dsus2**   **Esus4** **Dsus2**
All of me, ___ for ev'ry thirst ___ and

    A   **Dadd9/F♯** **Esus4** **Dsus2**
Ev'ry need. You ___ satisfy ___ me

       A/C♯ **Dsus2**
With Your love, ___ and all I have in You

Esus4
  Is more than enough.

Interlude 1 | **A** **Dadd9/F♯** | **Esus4** **Dsus2** | **A** **Dadd9/F♯** | **Esus4** **Dsus2** |

Verse 1

A   **Dsus2** **Esus4**   **A/C♯**
 You're my ___ supply, ___ my breath ___ of life,

Dsus2   **Bm7**   **Esus4**
 Still more awe - some than I know.

A   **Dsus2** **Esus4**   **A/C♯**
 You're my ___ reward ___ worth liv - ing for,

Dsus2   **Bm7**   **Esus4**
 Still more awe - some than I know.

Chorus 2   *Repeat Chorus 1*

Verse 2

> A   Dsus2 Esus4 A/C#
> You're my sac - rifice ____ of great - est price,

> Dsus2   Bm7   Esus4
> Still more awe - some than I know.

> A   Dsus2 Esus4   A/C#
> You're my com - ing King, ____ You are ev - 'rything,

> Dsus2   Bm7   Esus4
> Still more awe - some than I know.

Chorus 3

>   A Dadd9/F# Esus4 Dsus2
> All of You is more than enough ____ for

>   A Dsus2 Esus4 Dsus2
> All of me, ____ for ev'ry thirst ____ and

>   A   Dadd9/F# Esus4 Dsus2
> Ev'ry need. You ____ satisfy ____ me

>   A/C# Dsus2   Esus4
> With Your love, ____ and all I have in You

Bridge

>   A   Dsus2 Esus4   Dsus2
> ‖: More than all ____ I want, ____ more than all ____ I need,

> A/C# Dsus2   Esus4
>   You are more ____ than enough for me.

> A   Dsus2 Esus4   Dsus2
> More than all ____ I know, ____ more than all ____ I can,

> A/C# Dsus2   Esus4
>   You are more ____ than enough. :‖

Chorus 4

> *Repeat Chorus 1*

> | A   ‖

Every Move I Make

Words and Music by
David Ruis

Melody:

Ev - 'ry move I make, I make in

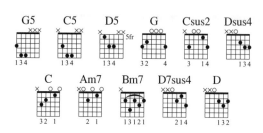

Intro

|G5 |C5 |D5 |C5 |

Chorus 1

G   Csus2   Dsus4   Csus2
Ev'ry move I make, I make in You; You make me ____ move, Jesus.

G   Csus2   Dsus4 Csus2
Ev'ry breath I take. I breathe in You.

G   C   Dsus4   Csus2
Ev'ry step I take, I take in You; You are my ____ way, Jesus.

G   C   Dsus4 C
Ev'ry breath I take, I breathe in You.

Interlude 1

‖: G5 |C5 |D5 |C5 :‖

Chorus 2 *Repeat Chorus 1*

Interlude 2 *Repeat Interlude 1*

Verse 1

```
G       Am7  Bm7      C   D7sus4
```
Waves of mercy, waves of grace,

```
G   Am7          Bm7    C   D7sus4
```
Ev'ry - where I look ____ I see ____ Your face.

```
G    Am7  Bm7      C   D7sus4
```
  Your love has captured me.

```
G    Am7           Bm7    C  D7sus4  G5  C5  D5  C5
```
Oh, my God, this love, ____ how can it   be?

Interlude 3   *Repeat Intro*

Chorus 3   *Repeat Chorus 1*

Interlude 4   *Repeat Interlude 1*

Verse 2   *Repeat Verse 1*

Interlude 5   *Repeat Intro*

Outro

```
       G      C       D       C
```
‖: La, la, la, la, la, la, la. La, la, la, la, la, la, la. :‖ *Repeat and fade*

Everyday

Words and Music by
Joel Houston

Melody:

What to say, _ Lord? It's   You who gave me life, _

(Capo 4th fret)

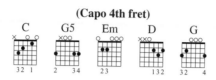

C   G5   Em   D   G

Intro
|C   G5 |Em   D |

Verse 1
C   G5   Em   D
What to say, Lord? It's   You who gave me life,

C   G5   Em   D
And I ___ can't ex - plain just how   much You mean to me, now.

C   G5   Em   D
That You would save me, Lord!   I give all that I am to You,

C   G5   Em   D   C G5 Em D
That ev'ry day I could   be a light that shines Your name.

Interlude 1   *Repeat Intro*

Verse 2
C   G5   Em   D
Ev'ry day, Lord, I   learn to stand upon Your Word,

C   G5   Em   D
And I pray that I,   I might come to know You more,

C   G5   Em   D
That You would guide me in ev'ry single step I take, yeah.

C   G5   Em   D   G
Ev'ry day I can   be a light unto the world.

Chorus 1	**C** **Em** **D** Ev'ry day ___ it's You I live for.

C   **Em**   **D**

Ev'ry day ___ it's You I live for.

G   **C**   **Em**   **D** **G**

  Ev'ry day, ___ I'll follow after You.

          C   **Em**   **D**   **G C Em D**

Ev'ry day ___ I'll walk with You, my Lord.

Interlude 2   ‖: **C**   **G5** |**Em**   **D**   :‖

Verse 3   *Repeat Verse 2*

Chorus 2   *Repeat Chorus 1*

Chorus 3   *Repeat Chorus 1*

Bridge

       G   **C**   **Em**   **D**

‖: It's You I live ___ for ev - 'ry day.

      G   **C**   **Em**   **D**

It's You I live ___ for ev - 'ry day.

      G   **C**   **Em**   **D G C Em D**

It's You I live ___ for ev - 'ry day.   :‖ *Play 4 times*

Chorus 4   *Repeat Chorus 1*

Chorus 5

G   **C**   **Em**   **D**

  Ev'ry day ___ it's You I   live for.

G   **C**   **Em** **D** **G**

  Ev'ry day, ___ I'll follow after You.

         C   **Em**   **D**

Ev'ry day ___ I'll walk with You.

   G

It's You I live for ev'ry day.

Firm Foundation

Words and Music by
Nancy Gordon and Jamie Harvill

Melody:

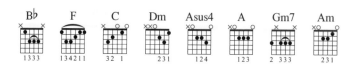

Je - sus, You're my firm foun - da - tion; _

Bb   F   C   Dm   Asus4   A   Gm7   Am

Intro	|**Bb** F |**C** Dm |**Bb** F |**C** F |

Chorus 1

F   Bb   F   C
Jesus, You're my firm foun-da - tion;

F   Bb   C
  I know I can stand ___ secure.

F   Bb   Asus4   A
Jesus, You're my firm foun-da - tion;

Bb   F   C   Dm
  I put my hope in Your ho - ly Word,

Bb   F   C   F
  I put my hope in Your ho - ly Word.

Verse 1

F
I have a living hope. (I have a living hope.)

Bb   C   F   Bb   C   F
I have a fu - ture. (I have a fu - ture.)

Dm   F
God has a plan for me. (God has a plan for me.)

Bb   Gm7   C
Of this I'm sure, of this I'm sure!

Chorus 2   *Repeat Chorus 1*

Verse 2

F
Your Word is faithful. (Your Word is faithful.)

B♭   **C** **F** **B♭**   **C** **F**
Mighty in pow-er. (Mighty in pow-er.)

Dm   **F**
God will deliver me. (God will deliver me.)

  B♭   **Gm7**   **C**
Of this I'm sure, of this I'm sure!

Chorus 3

F   **B♭**   **F** **C**
Jesus, You're my firm foun-da - tion;

F   **B♭**   **C**
  I know I can stand ___ secure.

F   **B♭**   **Asus4**   **A**
Jesus, You're my firm foun-da - tion;

B♭   **F**   **C**   **Dm**
  I put my hope in Your ho - ly Word,

B♭   **F**   **C**   **F**
  I put my hope in Your ho - ly Word.

B♭   **F**   **C**   **F** **Am7**
  I put my hope in Your ho - ly Word.

B♭   **F**   **C** **F**
  I put my hope in Your ho - ly Word.

Forever

Words and Music by
Chris Tomlin

Melody:

Give thanks to the Lord, _ our God and _ King. _

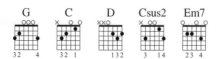

Verse 1

      G
Give thanks to the Lord, our God and King. His love endures forever.

C   **G**
For he is good, He is above all things. His love endures forev - er.

Chorus 1

D   **Csus2**   **D**   **Csus2**
Sing praise, sing praise. Sing praise, sing praise.

G   **Em7**
Forev - er God is faithful, forev - er God is strong,

D   **C**   **G**
Forev - er God is with us, forev - er, forev - er.

Verse 2

G
With a mighty hand and outstretched arm, His love endures forever.

C   **G**
   For the life that's been reborn, His love endures forev - er.

Chorus 2   *Repeat Chorus 1*

Verse 3

     G
   From the rising to the setting sun, His love endures forever.

         C   **G**
And by the grace of God we will carry on. His love endures forev - er.

Chorus 3   *Repeat Chorus 1*

Give Thanks

Words and Music by
Henry Smith

Melody:

Give thanks   with a grate-ful heart.

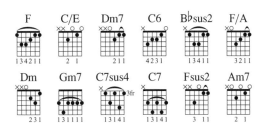

Intro

| F | C/E | Dm7 | C6 | |
| B♭sus2 | F/A Dm | Gm7 | C7sus4 C7 | |

Verse 1

    F   C/E   Dm7   C6
Give thanks with a grateful heart. Give thanks to the Holy One.

    B♭sus2   F/A Dm Gm7   C7sus4 C7
Give thanks because He's given Jesus Christ, His Son.

    F   C/E   Dm7   C6
Give thanks with a grateful heart. Give thanks to the Holy One.

    B♭sus2   F/A Dm Gm7   C7
Give thanks because He's given Jesus Christ, His Son.

Chorus 1

    Fsus2   Dm7   Gm7   C7   Am7
‖: And now let the weak say, "I am strong," let the poor say, "I am rich,"

    Dm7   Gm7 C7
Because of what the Lord has done for us. :‖

Verse 2   *Repeat Verse 1*

Chorus 2   *Repeat Chorus 1*

Outro

    B♭sus2   F
Give thanks. Give thanks.

Glorify Thy Name

Words and Music by
Donna Adkins

Melody:

Fa - ther, we   love   You, we

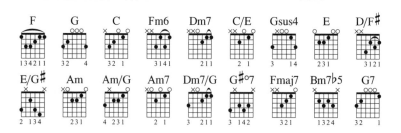

Intro |F |G |C |Fm6 |

Verse 1

      C   Dm7   G   C
Father, we love You, we praise You, we a - dore You,

      C/E   F   Gsus4 G
Glorify Thy name in all the earth.

Chorus 1

      C   F   E   D/F♯ E/G♯ Am Am/G
Glorify Thy name, glori - fy   Thy   name,

      F   G   C   Fm6
Glorify Thy name in all the earth.

	C Dm7 G C
Verse 2	Jesus, we love You, we praise You, we a - dore You,

C/E   F   Gsus4 G
Glorify Thy name in all the earth.

Chorus 2	*Repeat Chorus 1*

	Am7 Dm7 Dm7/G G#°7 Am7
Verse 3	Spirit, we ___ love you, we praise You, we a - dore You,

C/E   Fmaj7   Gsus4 Bm7♭5 E
Glorify Thy ___ name in all the earth.

	Am7 Dm7 E D/F# E/G# Am Am/G
Chorus 3	Glorify Thy name, glori - fy Thy name,

F   G   C   G7
Glorify Thy name in all the earth.

	C F E D/F# E/G# Am Am/G
Chorus 4	Glorify Thy name, glori - fy Thy name,

F   G   C
Glorify Thy name in all the earth.

God Is Good All the Time

Words and Music by
Don Moen and Paul Overstreet

Melody:

God is good all the time.

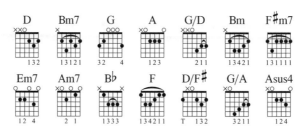

| D | Bm7 | G | A | G/D | Bm | F#m7 |
| Em7 | Am7 | Bb | F | D/F# | G/A | Asus4 |

Chorus 1

>   D   Bm7
> God is good all the time.
>
>   G   A
> He put a song of praise in this   heart of mine.
>
>   D   Bm7
> God is good all the time.
>
>   G   A
> Through the darkest night, His light will shine.
>
>   G   A   D   G/D   D
> God is good, God is good all the time.

Verse 1

>   A   Bm
> If you're walkin' through the valley,
>
>   G   Bm   A
> there are shadows all a - round.
>
>   F#m7   Bm
> Do not fear, He will guide you.
>
>   G   A
> He will keep you safe and sound,
>
>   Em7   A
> For He has promised to never leave ____ you
>
>   Em7   G   A
> Or for - sake you, and His Word is true.

Chorus 2   *Repeat Chorus 1*

     A   Bm
Verse 2 We were sinners and so un - worthy.

     G   Bm A
    Still, for us He chose to die.

     F#m7   Bm
    He filled us with His Holy Spirit.

     G   A
    Now we can stand and testify

    Em7   A   Em7   G A
    That His love is everlast - ing and His mercies, they will never end.

Chorus 3 *Repeat Chorus 1*

    Bm   F#m7 Am7   Em7
Bridge Though I may not understand ___ all the plans You have for me,

    Bb   F   Em7 D/F# G G/A
    My life is in Your hands, and through the eyes of faith I can clearly see…

    D   Bm7
Chorus 4 God is good all the time.

    G   A
    He put a song of praise in this heart of mine.

    D   Bm7
    God is good all the time.

     G   A
    Through the darkest night, His light will shine.

    G   A   G   A
    God is good, God is good, God is good, He's so good,

    Em7   Asus4 A D G/D D
    God is good, He's so good all the time.

God of Wonders

Words and Music by
Marc Byrd and Steve Hindalong

Lord of all __ cre-a - tion, __

Dsus4   Em   Csus2   G   D   Am7   C

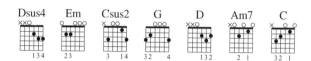

Verse 1

      Dsus4   Em   Csus2
      Lord of all ____ crea - tion,

      Dsus4   Em   Csus2
      Of water, earth ____ and ____ sky,

      Dsus4   Em   Csus2
      The heavens are Your taberna - cle;

      Dsus4   Em   Csus2
      Glory to the Lord ____ on ____ high.

Chorus 1

      G   D   Am7   Csus2
      God of wonders beyond our galax-y, You are holy,   holy.

        G   D   Am7   Csus2
      The universe declares Your majes-ty. You are holy,   holy.

      Lord of heaven and earth, Lord of heaven and earth.

Interlude	‖: **Dsus4** **Em** |**Csus2** :‖

Verse 2

Dsus4   **Em**   **Csus2**
Early in ____ the morn - ing

Dsus4   **Em**   **Csus2**
I will celebrate ____ the ____ light.

Dsus4   **Em**   **Csus2**
And I will stumble in the dark - ness,

Dsus4   **Em**   **Csus2**
I will call Your name ____ by ____ night.

Chorus 2   *Repeat Chorus 1*

Outro

Am7   **C**
Hallelujah to the Lord of heaven and earth.

Am7   **C**
Hallelujah to the Lord of heaven and earth.

Am7   **C**   **G**
Hallelujah to the Lord of heaven and earth.

Great Is the Lord

Words and Music by
Michael W. Smith and Deborah D. Smith

Great is the Lord. He is ho - ly and just,

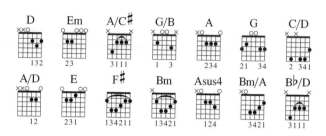

Intro   ‖: D | :‖ ***Play 4 times***

Verse 1

   D Em
Great is the Lord.

   A/C♯ D
He is holy and just,

   G/B   A   G D
By the power we trust in His love.

     Em
Great is the Lord,

   A/C♯   D
He is faithful and true,

   G/B   A   G D
By His mercy He proves He is love.

Chorus 1

C/D   G D
Great is the Lord, and worthy of glory,

C/D   A/D D
Great is the Lord, and worthy of praise.

C/D   E   A
Great is the Lord, now lift up your voice,

 F#   Bm
Now lift up your voice:

Em G Asus4 A Bm Bm/A
Great _____ is the Lord!

Em G Asus4 A D
Great _____ is the Lord!

Verse 2   *Repeat Verse 1*

Chorus 2   *Repeat Chorus 1*

Chorus 3

C/D   G D
Great are You, Lord, and worthy of glory,

C/D   A/D D
Great are You, Lord, and worthy of praise.

C/D   E   A
Great are You, Lord, I lift up my voice,

 F#   Bm
I lift up my voice:

Em G Asus4 A Bm Bm/A
Great _____ are You, Lord!

Em G Asus4 A D
Great _____ are You, Lord!

     Bb/D
Great are You, Lord!

     C/D
Great are You, Lord!

     D A D A D A D A D
Great are You, Lord!

Hallelujah
(Your Love Is Amazing)

Words and Music by
Brenton Brown and Brian Doerksen

Melody:

Your love is ___ a-maz - ing,

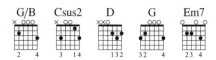

G/B   Csus2   D   G   Em7

                  G/B   Csus2

Verse 1   Your love is amaz - ing, steady and unchang - ing.

                        D   Csus2

           Your love is a moun - tain firm beneath my feet.

                  G/B   Csus2

           Your love is a mys - t'ry, how You gently lift ___ me.

                        D   Csus2

           When I am surround - ed Your love carries me.

               G   D   Em7   Csus2

Chorus 1   ‖: Hallelu - jah, hallelu - jah, hallelu - jah,   Your love makes me sing.   :‖

                  G/B   Csus2

Verse 2   Your love is surpris - ing, I can feel it ris - ing,

                        D   Csus2

           All the joy that's grow - ing deep inside of me.

                  G/B   Csus2

           Ev'ry time I see ___ You all Your goodness shines ___ through,

                      D   Csus2

           I can feel this God ___ song rising up in me.

Chorus 2   *Repeat Chorus 1*

Verse 3   *Repeat Verse 1*

Chorus 3   *Repeat Chorus 1*

           Csus2

Outro   Lord, You make me sing. How You make me sing.

He Is Exalted

Words and Music by
Twila Paris

Melody:

He is ex - al - ted, the King is ex - al - ted on __

(Capo 3rd fret)

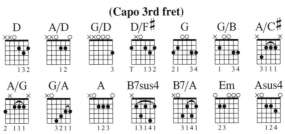

Intro

‖: D   A/D | G/D A/D :‖

Verse 1

D   D/F♯   G   G/B A/C♯
He is exalted, the King is exalted on high. I will praise Him.

D   D/F♯
He is exalted, for - ever exalted

    G   A/G   G/A   A B7sus4 B7/A
And I   will   praise His name.

Chorus 1

Em D   A/C♯   D   D/F♯   G   D/F♯
He   is the Lord, for - ever His truth shall reign.

Em D   A/C♯   D   D/F♯ G   D/F♯
Heav - en and earth re - joice in His holy   name.

Em   D/F♯   G   Asus4 D A/D G/D A/D
He is ex - alted, the King is ex - alted on high.

Interlude 1

| D   A/D | G/D A/D |

Verse 2

Repeat Verse 1

Chorus 2

Repeat Chorus 1

Interlude 2

Repeat Interlude 1

Chorus 3

Repeat Chorus 1

Outro

| D   A/D | G/D A/D | D   ‖

He Has Made Me Glad

Words and Music by
Leona Von Brethorst

Melody:

I will en-ter His gates _ with thanks -

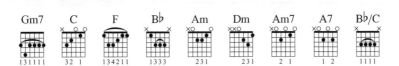

Gm7 C F Bb Am Dm Am7 A7 Bb/C

Intro
| Gm7   C | F   Bb   F |

Verse 1

C   F   Bb   Am Dm Gm7
I will enter His gates with thanks - giving in my heart,

C   F   Bb   Am7 Dm Gm7
I will enter His courts with praise.

C   F   Bb   F   A7 Dm
I will say this is the day ____ that the Lord has   made.

 Gm7   C   F Bb F C
I will rejoice for He has made me glad.

Chorus 1

F   Bb   F   A7   Dm
He has made me glad, He has made me glad.

 Gm7   C   F Gm7 Am7 C
I will rejoice for He has made me glad.

F   Bb   F   A7   Dm
He has made me glad, He has made me glad.

 Gm7   C   F Bb F
I will rejoice for He has made me glad.

GUITAR CHORD SONGBOOK

Verse 2

B♭/C F   B♭   Am Dm Gm7
I have entered Your gates with thanks - giving in my heart,

C   F   B♭   Am7 Dm Gm7
I have entered Your courts with praise.

C   F   B♭   F   A7 Dm
I will say, "This is the day ___ that the Lord has made!"

 Gm7   C   F B♭ F C
I will rejoice for You have made me glad.

Chorus 2

F   B♭ F   A7   Dm
You have made me glad, You have made me glad.

 Gm7   C   F Gm7 Am7 C
I will rejoice for You have made me glad.

F   B♭ F   A7   Dm
You have made me glad, You have made me glad.

 Gm7   C   F B♭ F B♭/C
I will rejoice, for You have made me glad.

Chorus 3   *Repeat Chorus 1*

The Heart of Worship

Words and Music by
Matt Redman

Melody:

When the mu-sic fades, ___ all is stripped a - way, _

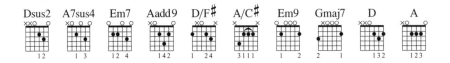

Dsus2 A7sus4 Em7 Aadd9 D/F♯ A/C♯ Em9 Gmaj7 D A

Intro | Dsus2 | A7sus4 | Em7 | A7sus4 |

Verse 1
Dsus2   Aadd9
When the music fades, ___ all is stripped away,

Em7   A7sus4
And I simply come,

Dsus2   Aadd9
Longing to bring ___ something that's of worth

Em7   A7sus4
That will bless Your heart.

Pre-Chorus 1
Em7   D/F♯   A7sus4
I'll bring You more than a song,

                    Em7   D/F♯   A7sus4
For a song in itself   is not what You have required.

Em7   D/F♯
You search much deeper within

A7sus4
Through the way things appear;

Em7   D/F♯   A7sus4
You're looking into my heart.

Chorus 1

Dsus2   A/C♯
I'm coming back to the heart ___ of worship,

        Em9   D/F♯ Gmaj7   A7sus4
And it's all about You,   all about You, ___ Jesus.

Dsus2   A/C♯
I'm sorry, Lord, for the thing ___ I've made it,

        Em9   D/F♯ Gmaj7   A7sus4
When it's all about You,   all about You, ___ Jesus.

Interlude 1

| Dsus2 | D   A | Em7 | A7sus4 | |

Verse 2

Dsus2   Aadd9
King of endless worth, ___ no one could express

Em7   A7sus4
How much You deserve.

Dsus2   Aadd9
Though I'm weak and poor, ___ all I have is Yours,

Em7   A7sus4
Ev'ry single breath.

Pre-Chorus 2   *Repeat Pre-Chorus 1*

Chorus 2   *Repeat Chorus 1*

| D   ‖

Here I Am to Worship

Words and Music by
Tim Hughes

Melody:

Light of the World, You stepped down in - to dark - ness,

| E | Bsus4 | Asus2 | F#m | B/D# | E/G# | A |

Intro

|E   Bsus4 |Asus2 |E   Bsus4 |Asus2 |

Verse 1

E   Bsus4   F#m
Light of the World, You stepped down into darkness,

E   Bsus4   Asus2
Opened my eyes, let me ____ see.

E   Bsus4   F#m
Beauty that made this heart adore You,

E   Bsus4   Asus2
Hope of a life spent with ____ You.

Chorus 1

                E   B/D#
Here I am to worship, here I am to bow down,

        E/G#   Asus2
Here I am to say that You're my God.

                    E   B/D#
You're altogether lovely, altogether worthy,

        E/G#   Asus2
Altogether wonderful to me.

|Bsus4 |

Verse 2	E Bsus4 F#m King of all days, oh, so highly exalted,

E   Bsus4   Asus2
King of all days, oh, so highly exalted,

Verse 2

E   Bsus4   F#m
King of all days, oh, so highly exalted,

E   Bsus4   Asus2
Glorious in heaven a - bove.

E   Bsus4   F#m
Humbly You came to the earth You created,

E   Bsus4   Asus2
All for love's sake became ___ poor.

Chorus 2   *Repeat Chorus 1*

Bridge

              B/D#   E/G#   A   Asus2
‖: And I'll nev - er know ___ how much ___ it cost

          B/D#   E/G#   A   Asus2
To see ___ my sin ___ upon ___ that cross. :‖

Chorus 3   *Repeat Chorus 1*

| Bsus4 | E   ‖

Holiness

Words and Music by
Scott Underwood

Melody:

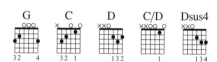

Ho - li - ness, __ ho - li - ness __

G   C   D   C/D   Dsus4

Intro |G   C |D |G   C |D   C |

Verse 1
G   C   D   C
Holiness, ___ holiness ___ is what I long ___ for.

G   C   D   C
Holiness ___ is what I need.

G   C   D
Holiness, ___ holiness

          C   G   C   D   C/D
Is what You want from me.

Chorus 1
          G   C   D
So take my heart ___ and form it.

          G   C   D
Take my mind, ___ trans - form it.

          G   C   D   G   C   D
Take my will, ___ con - form it to Yours, ___ to Yours, ___ O Lord.

Verse 2

```
        G                C              D                C
        Faithfulness, __ faithfulness __ is what I long ___ for.

        G              C            D   C
        Faithfulness __ is what I need.

        G              C              D
        Faithfulness, __ faithfulness

                    C           G   C   D   C/D
        Is what You want from me.
```

Chorus 2   *Repeat Chorus 1*

Verse 3

```
        G                C              D                C
        Brokenness, __ brokenness ___ is what I long ___ for.

        G              C            D   C
        Brokenness __ is what I need.

        G              C              D
        Brokenness, __ brokenness

                    C           G   C   D   C/D
        Is what You want from me.
```

Chorus 3   *Repeat Chorus 1*

Outro

```
                    G            C   D
        To Yours, ___ to Yours, ___ O Lord.

                    G            C   Dsus4  D   C/D   G
        To Yours, ___ to Yours, ___ O Lord.     O     Lord.
```

Holy and Anointed One

Words and Music by
John Barnett

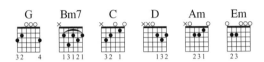

Chorus 1

G Bm7 C   G   D   C
Je - sus,   Je - sus,

G   D   C   Am   G D G
Holy and ___ Anoint - ed One,   Je - sus.

Chorus 2   *Repeat Chorus 1*

Verse 1

                              C   G
Your name is like hon - ey on my lips.

                    C   G
Your Spirit is wa - ter to my soul.

                         C   Em
Your Word is a lamp ___ unto my feet.

                 C   D
Jesus, I love ___ You. I love You.

Chorus 3

```
G  Bm7  C    G   D   C
Je  -   sus, Je  -   sus,

G        D       C      Am   G   D   G
Risen and ___  Exalt - ed One,  Je  -  sus.
```

Verse 2   *Repeat Verse 1*

Verse 3
```
                    C                G
Your name is like hon - ey on my lips.

                  C              G
Your Spirit is wa - ter to my soul.

                     C             Em
Your Word is a lamp ___ unto my feet.

                C            D
Jesus, I love ___ You. I love You.
```

Outro
```
   G  Bm7  C    G   D   C
‖: Je  -   sus, Je  -   sus. :‖
 | G         ‖
```

How Majestic Is Your Name

Words and Music by
Michael W. Smith

Melody:

O   Lord, _our Lord, _ how ma - jes - tic   is   Your

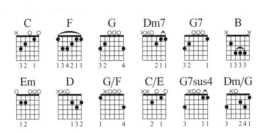

C   F   G   Dm7   G7   B
Em   D   G/F   C/E   G7sus4   Dm/G

Intro

| C | F | C | G C |
| | F | C | G C |

Chorus 1

    C   F   C   G   C
O Lord, our Lord, how ma - jestic is Your name in all the earth.

                                   F   C   G
O Lord, our Lord, how ma - jestic is Your name in all the earth.

Verse 1

   F C Dm7 G   G7 C
O Lord, _____ we praise Your name.

   F C Dm7 G   C
O Lord, _____ we magnify Your name,

  B   Em   D   G   G/F
Prince of Peace, Mighty God,

   C/E F   G7   C F C G C
O   Lord God Al - might - y.

Chorus 2   *Repeat Chorus 1*

Verse 2

    F **C** **Dm7** **G**   **G7** **C**
O Lord, _____ we praise Your name.

    F **C** **Dm7** **G**   **C**
O Lord, _____ we magnify Your name,

B   **Em**   **D**   **G** **G/F**
Prince of Peace, Mighty God,

   C/E **F**   **G7**   **C** **F** **C** **G** **C**
O Lord God Al - might - y.

B   **Em**   **D**   **G** **G/F**
Prince of Peace, Mighty God,

   C/E **F**   **G7sus4** **G** **C**
O Lord God Al - might - y.

Outro

F	**C**	**F**	**C**	
F	**C**	**G** **Dm/G**	**C**	‖

Hungry
(Falling on My Knees)

Words and Music by
Kathryn Scott

Hun-gry, I ____ come to ____ You,

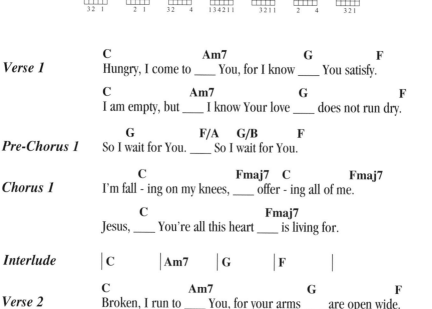

Verse 1

C   Am7   G   F
Hungry, I come to ____ You, for I know ____ You satisfy.

C   Am7   G   F
I am empty, but ____ I know Your love ____ does not run dry.

Pre-Chorus 1

  G   F/A G/B   F
So I wait for You. ____ So I wait for You.

Chorus 1

     C   Fmaj7 C   Fmaj7
I'm fall - ing on my knees, ____ offer - ing all of me.

     C   Fmaj7
Jesus, ____ You're all this heart ____ is living for.

Interlude

| C | Am7 | G | F | |

Verse 2

C   Am7   G   F
Broken, I run to ____ You, for your arms ____ are open wide.

C   Am7   G   F
I am weary, but ____ I know Your touch ____ restores my life.

Pre-Chorus 2 *Repeat Pre-Chorus 1*

Chorus 2 *Repeat Chorus 1*

| C | Fmaj7 | |

Outro

     C   Fmaj7 C   Fmaj7
I'm fall - ing on my knees, ____ offer - ing all of me.

     C   Fmaj7   C
Jesus, ____ You're all this heart ____ is living for.

I Give You My Heart

Words and Music by
Reuben Morgan

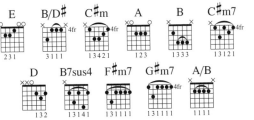

Verse 1

 E   B/D♯ C♯m A E B
This is my desi - re, to hon - or You.

C♯m7   B/D♯ E   D A B7sus4
Lord, with all my ___ heart ___ I worship You.

E   B/D♯ C♯m A E B
All I have within ___ me, I give You praise.

C♯m7 B/D♯   D A B7sus4
All that I a - dore is in You.

Chorus 1

 E   B   F♯m7
 Lord, I give You my heart, ___ I give You my soul.

 B7sus4
I live for You alone.

 E   B/D♯   F♯m7
 Ev'ry breath that I take, ___ ev'ry moment I'm awake,

 B7sus4   E G♯m7 A/B
Lord, have Your way in me.

Verse 2   *Repeat Verse 1*

Chorus 2

 E   B   F♯m7
 Lord, I give You my heart, ___ I give You my soul.

 B7sus4
I live for You alone.

 E   B/D♯   F♯m7
 Ev'ry breath that I take, ___ ev'ry moment I'm awake,

 B7sus4   E G♯m7 A/B
Lord, have Your way in me.

Chorus 3   *Repeat Chorus 2*

I Could Sing of Your Love Forever

Words and Music by
Martin Smith

O - ver __ the moun - tains and __ the sea

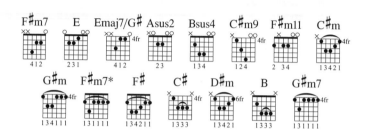

Intro

‖: F#m7 | | E | :‖

Verse 1

E   Emaj7/G#
Over the mountains and the sea   Your river runs with love for me.

F#m7   Asus2   Bsus4
And I will open my heart ___and let the healer set me free.

E   Emaj7/G#
I'm happy to be in the truth   and I will daily lift my hands.

F#m7   Asus2   Bsus4
For I will always sing of when Your love came down.

Chorus 1

E   Bsus4
I could sing of Your love ___ forever,

C#m9   Asus2   Bsus4
I could sing of Your love _____ for - ever.

E   Bsus4
I could sing of Your love ___ forever,

C#m9   Asus2   Bsus4
I could sing of Your love _____ for - ever.

Verse 2	*Repeat Verse 1*
Chorus 2	*Repeat Chorus 1*

Bridge

F#m11   Asus2   C#m   G#m
Oh, I feel like danc - ing;   it's foolishness, I know.

F#m7*   Asus2
But when the world has seen ___ the light,

                  Bsus4
They will dance ___ with joy like we're dancing now.

Chorus 3	*Repeat Chorus 1*

Chorus 4

F#   C#
I could sing of Your love ___ forever,

D#m   B   C#
I could sing of Your love ___ for - ever.

F#   C#
I could sing of Your love ___ forever,

D#m   B   C#
I could sing of Your love ___ for - ever.

Outro | G#m7 | | F# | ‖

I Love to Be in Your Presence

Words and Music by
Paul Baloche and Ed Kerr

Melody:

I love to be ___ in Your pres - ence,

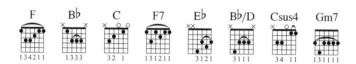

F	Bb	C	F7	Eb	Bb/D	Csus4	Gm7
134211	1333	32 1	131211	3121	3111	34 11	131111

Chorus 1

    F   Bb
I love to be in Your pres - ence,

            F   C
With Your peo - ple singing prais - es.

    F   F7   Bb
I love to stand ___ and rejoice,

         F   C   F
Lift my hands ___ and raise ___ my voice.

Chorus 2   *Repeat Chorus 1*

Verse 1

Bb   F   Bb   F
  You set my feet to dancing,   You fill my heart with song.

Eb   Bb/D   Csus4   C
  You give me reason to rejoice, ___ rejoice.

Chorus 3   *Repeat Chorus 1*

Outro

Gm7 F   Bb   F   Gm7 F   C   F
Lift my hands, lift my hands, lift my hands and raise ___ my voice.

I Love You Lord

Words and Music by
Laurie Klein

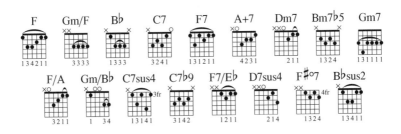

Verse 1

    F   **Gm/F F**
I love You, Lord, and I lift   my voice

  B♭ **F** **C7**   **F**   **C7**
To wor - ship You. O my soul, rejoice!

       F   **Gm/F F**
Take joy, my King, in what   You hear.

F7   **B♭**   **F**   **C7**   **F B♭ F**
May it be a sweet, sweet sound in Your ear.

Verse 2

    F   **A+7**   **Dm7**   **Bm7♭5**
I love You, Lord, ___ and I lift my voice

    Gm7 **F/A** **Gm/B♭** **Bm7♭5** **C7sus4**   **C7♭9**
To   wor - ship You.   O my _____ soul, re - joice!

      F   **F7/E♭** **D7sus4** **Dm7** **Bm7♭5**
Take joy, my King, ___ in what You ___ hear.

F♯°7   **Gm7** **F/A** **B♭sus2** **C7**   **B♭** **F**
May it be a sweet, sweet sound in Your ___ ear.

Verse 3   *Repeat Verse 1*

I Stand in Awe

Words and Music by
Mark Altrogge

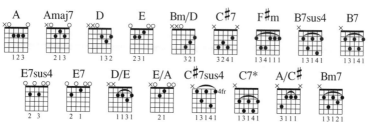

Verse 1

        A   Amaj7
You are beautiful beyond de - scription,

       D   A
Too marvelous for words,

             D   A
Too wonderful for compre - hen - sion,

      D   E Bm/D C#7
Like nothing ever seen or heard.

Pre-Chorus 1

      F#m   B7sus4   B7
Who can grasp Your infinite wisdom?

      D   E
Who can fathom the depth of Your love?

      A   Amaj7
You are beautiful beyond de - scription,

      D   E7sus4 E7 A   D/E
Majes - ty en - throned a - bove.

Chorus

    E   A   E/A   D
And I stand, I stand in awe of You.

    A   E/A   D
I stand, I stand in awe of You.

    C#7sus4 C#7*   D
Holy God, to   whom all praise is due,

 A/C# Bm7   E7   A
  I   stand in awe of You.

I Will Exalt Your Name

Words and Music by
Jeffrey B. Scott

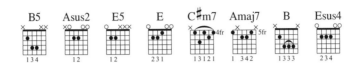

Intro

| B5   Asus2 | E5 | | B5   Asus2 | E5 | |

Chorus 1

       B5   Asus2   E
I will exalt _____ Your name.

       B5   Asus2   E
I will exalt _____ Your name.

       B5   Asus2   E   B5
I will exalt _____ Your name, ___ oh, my God.

Chorus 2

Asus2   B5   Asus2   E
I will exalt _____ Your name.

      B5   Asus2   E
I will exalt _____ Your name.

      B5   Asus2   E   B5
I will exalt _____ Your name, ___ oh, my God.

Verse 1

     C#m7   Amaj7   B   E   Esus4   E
Never before, _____ never again,

      C#m7   Amaj7   B   E
Will there be one _____ like You.

Chorus 3   *Repeat Chorus 1*

Chorus 4   *Repeat Chorus 1*

Outro

     Asus2   E
I will ex - alt Your name.

I Want to Know You

Words and Music by
Andy Park

Melody:

In the se - cret, in the qui - et place, ___

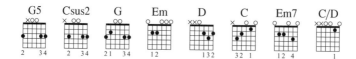

| G5 | Csus2 | G | Em | D | C | Em7 | C/D |

Intro　　　‖: G5 　│　　│ Csus2 　│　　:‖

Verse 1

G　　　　　　　　　　　　　Csus2
In the secret, in the quiet place,

Em　　　　　D　　　Csus2
In the stillness You are there.

G　　　　　　　　　　　　C
In the secret, in the quiet ho - ur I wait only for You,

Em7　　　　　D　　　C
'Cause I want to know You more.

```
                    G           D         Em        C
Chorus 1            I want to know You,    I want to hear Your voice.

                    G           D             Csus2
                    I want to know You more.

                    G           D         Em        C
                    I want to touch You,    I want to see Your face.

                    G           D             Csus2
                    I want to know You more.

                    G                             Csus2
Verse 2             I am reaching for the highest goal,

                    Em7             D         Csus2
                    that I might re - ceive the prize.

                    G                             C
                    Pressing onward, pushing ev'ry hin - d'rance aside, out of my way,

                    Em7             D         C
                    'Cause I want to know You more.
```

Chorus 2   *Repeat Chorus 1*

| C   C/D |

Chorus 3   *Repeat Chorus 1*

It Is You

Words and Music by
Peter Furler

Melody:

As we lift up our hands, _ will You meet us here? _

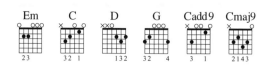

Em   C   D   G   Cadd9   Cmaj9

Verse 1

Em   C   D
As we lift up our hands, will You meet us here?

Em   C   D
As we call out Your name, will You meet us here?

Em   C   D
We have come to this place to worship You,

Em   C   D
God of mercy and grace.

Chorus 1

G   Cadd9   G   Cadd9
It is You ___ we adore. ___ It is You ___ praises are for,

G   Cadd9   G   Cmaj9
Only You.   The heavens declare ___ it is You, ___ it is You.

D   C   G
‖: And holy, holy is our   God Al - mighty,

D   C   G
And holy, holy is His   name a - lone, :‖

Cadd9   G   Cadd9
It is You we adore. ___ It is You, ___ only You.

Verse 2   *Repeat Verse 1*

Chorus 2

           G   **Cadd9**   **G**   **Cadd9**
It is You ___ we adore. ___ It is You ___ praises are for,

          G   **Cadd9**   **G**   **Cmaj9**
Only You.   The heavens declare ___ it is You, ___ it is You.

  D   **C**   **G**
‖: And holy, holy is our   God Al - mighty,

D   **C**   **G**
 And holy, holy is His   name a - lone, :‖

Bridge

          D   **C**   **G**
‖: As we lift up our hands, as we call ___ on Your name,

          D   **C**   **G**
Will You vis - it this place by Your mer - cy and grace? :‖

Chorus 3

G   **Cadd9**   **G**   **Cmaj9**
It is You we adore. ___ It is You. ___ It is You.

  D   **C**   **G**
‖: And holy, holy is our   God Al - mighty,

D   **C**   **G**
 And holy, holy is His   name a - lone, :‖ *Play 3 times*

Outro

G   **C**   **G**   **C**
It is You we adore. ___ It is You, ___ only You.

Jesus, Lover of My Soul

Words and Music by John Ezzy,
Daniel Grul and Stephen McPherson

Melody:

It's all a-bout You, ___

F#m9   D   A   E/G#   F#m   E

131111 132 123 2 134 134111 231

Dsus2   F#m7   Esus4   A/C#   Asus2

13   131111   234   3111   12

Chorus 1

       F#m9 D A E/G#
It's all about You, _____ Jesus,

      F#m9 D   A   E/G#
And all this is for ___ You, for Your glory and Your fame.

      F#m9 D A   D
It's not about me as if You should do things my ___ way.

F#m   E   Dsus2 A   D F#m7 E
You alone are God ___ and I surren - der to Your ___ ways.

Verse 1

A Dsus2 E   A
Je - sus, lover of my soul,

D   A   E Esus4 E
All consuming fire ___ is in Your ___ gaze.

A D E   A
Je - sus, I want You to know,

D   A   E Esus4 E
I will follow You ___ all my ___ days.

  A/C#   Dsus2 F#m7   D
For no one else in history is like You,

   A   E   D
And history itself ___belongs to You.

A/C#   Dsus2   F#m9 D
Alpha and Ome - ga, You have loved ___ me,

   A   D   E Esus4 E
And I will share eter - nity with ___ You.

Chorus 2   *Repeat Chorus 1*

Interlude | A | D | F#m7 | E/G# |

                                   F#m9   D   A   E/G#
Chorus 3   It's all about ____ You,   Jesus,

                                        F#m9   D   A   E
                      And all this is for ____ You,   for Your glory and Your fame.

                                        F#m9   D   A   D
                      It's not about ____ me   as if You should do things my ____ way.

                      F#m   E/G#   D
                      You alone are God ____ and I surren - der.

                      D   F#m9   D   A   E/G#
Chorus 4   It's all about ____ You,   Jesus,

                                        F#m9   D   A   E
                      And all this is for ____ You,   for Your glory and Your fame.

                                        F#m9   D   A   D
                      It's not about ____ me   as if You should do things my ____ way.

                      F#m   E/G#   D   A   D
                      You alone are God ____ and I surren - der to Your ____ ways.

Outro | F#m7 | E/G# | A | Dsus2 |
                      | F#m7 | E/G# | Asus2   ‖

Jesus, Name Above All Names

Words and Music by
Naida Hearn

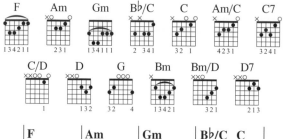

Intro
| F | Am | Gm | Bb/C C |

Chorus 1
   F   Am
Jesus, name above all names,

        Gm   C Bb/C Am/C C7
Beautiful Savior, glorious Lord.

     F   Am
Em - manuel, God is with us,

          Gm   C   C7   F   Bb/C C
Blessed Re - deemer, ____ living word.

Chorus 2
   F   Am
Jesus, name above all names,

        Gm   C Bb/C Am/C C7
Beautiful Savior, glorious Lord.

      F   Am
Em-manuel, God is with us,

         Gm   C   C7   F   C/D D
Blessed Re - deemer, ____ living word.

Chorus 3
   G   Bm
Jesus, name above all names,

        Am   D C/D Bm/D D7
Beautiful Savior, glorious Lord.

     G   Bm
Em - manuel, God is with us,

        Am   D   D7 C G
Blessed Re - deemer, ____ living word.

More Love, More Power

Words and Music by
Eddie Espinosa

Melody:

More love, _ more pow- er,

(Capo 3rd fret)

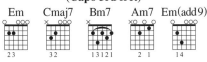

Em   Cmaj7   Bm7   Am7   Em(add9)

Intro

| Em | Cmaj7 | Bm7 | Em Bm7 | Em Bm7 |

Chorus 1

    Em   Cmaj7   Bm7   Em
More love,   more power,   more of You in my ___ life.

            Cmaj7   Bm7   Em
More love,   more power,   more of You in my ___ life.

Verse 1

            Am7   Em
And I will worship You with all of my heart,

            Am7   Em
And I will worship You with all of my mind,

            Am7   Em
And I will worship You with all of my strength,

              Cmaj7 Bm7
For You are my Lord.

Chorus 2   *Repeat Chorus 1*

Verse 2   *Repeat Verse 1*

Verse 3

            Am7   Em
And I will sing Your praise with all my heart,

            Am7   Em
And I will sing Your praise with all of my mind,

            Am7   Em
And I will sing Your praise with all of my strength,

              Cmaj7
For You are my Lord,

Bm7   Cmaj7   Bm7   Em(add9)
For You are my Lord, ___   You are my Lord.

Knowing You
(All I Once Held Dear)

Words and Music by
Graham Kendrick

Melody:

All I _____ once held _____ dear,

Am	F	C	C/E	G	G/B	Gsus4	Em/G	G/F	F/A
231	134211	32 1	2 1	32 4	2 4	3 11	312	1 4	3211

Verse 1

   Am F   C   C/E   F G C
All I once held dear, built my life up - on,

   G/B Am F   C   Am   Gsus4 G
All this   world re - veres and wars to own,

C/E F   G   C C/E F   G C
All I once thought gain I have count - ed loss,

   G/B Am   F   C   Am   Gsus4 G
Spent and   worth - less now com - pared to this.

Chorus 1

C/E   F   C   F G   C
Knowing You, Jesus,   knowing You.

   Am Em/G F   G/F
There is no greater   thing.

         C/E   F/A
You're my all, You're the best,

         C   F
You're my joy, my righteousness;

       C/E   F/A C G
And I love You, Lord.

Verse 2

      Am   F   C C/E   F   G   C
Now my heart's de - sire is to   know You more,

    G/B Am F C   Am   Gsus4 G
To be   found in You and know as Yours,

C/E   F   G C C/E   F   G C
To all pos - sess by faith what I could not earn,

    G/B Am F C   Am   Gsus4 G
All sur - pass-ing gift of righteous - ness.

Chorus 2

Repeat Chorus 1

Verse 3

     Am F   C   C/E   F G C
Oh, to know the pow'r of Your ris - en life,

    G/B Am F   C   Am   Gsus4 G
And to   know You in Your suffer - ing,

C/E F   G   C C/E   F   G C
To be - come like You in Your death, my Lord,

    G/B Am   F   C   Am Gsus4 G
So with You to   live and never die.

Chorus 3

C/E   F   C   F G   C
Knowing You, Jesus,   knowing You.

     Am Em/G   F   G/F
There is no greater   thing.

        C/E   F/A
You're my all, You're the best,

        C   F
You're my joy, my righteousness;

     C/E   F/A C Gsus4 G C
And I love You, Lord.

Lamb of God

Words and Music by
Twila Paris

Melody:

Your on-ly Son, no sin to hide,

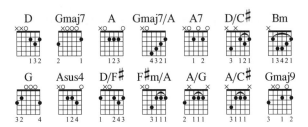

D Gmaj7 A Gmaj7/A A7 D/C# Bm

G Asus4 D/F# F#m/A A/G A/C# Gmaj9

Intro
| D   Gmaj7   A | D |

Verse 1

      Gmaj7/A D   A7 D
Your only   Son, no sin to hide,

     D/C# Bm   G   Asus4 A
But You have sent Him from Your side

     D/F#   G   F#m/A Bm G
To walk up - on the guilty   sod

          D/F#   Gmaj7/A D
And to be - come the Lamb   of   God.

Verse 2

      Gmaj7/A D   A7   D
Your gift of   love they cruci - fied,

     D/C#   Bm   G   Asus4 A
They laughed and scorned Him as He died.

     D/F# G   F#m/A Bm   G
The humble King they named a fraud

         D/F#   Gmaj7 A D
And sacri - ficed the Lamb   of   God.

Chorus 1

D/F♯   Bm   Gmaj7 A/G D/F♯
O Lamb of God, sweet Lamb   of   God,

D A/C♯ Bm Gmaj9 Asus4 A
I love the   holy Lamb of God.

D/F♯   G   F♯m/A Bm
O wash me in His precious blood,

D   Gmaj7/A A7   D
My Jesus Christ, the Lamb   of   God.

Verse 3

Gmaj7/A D   A7   D
I was so   lost I should have died,

D/C♯   Bm   G   Asus4 A
But You have brought me to Your side

D/F♯ G   F♯m/A Bm G
To be led by Your staff and rod

D/F♯   Gmaj7 A D
And to be called a Lamb   of God.

Chorus 2   *Repeat Chorus 1*

Let Everything that Has Breath

Words and Music by
Matt Redman

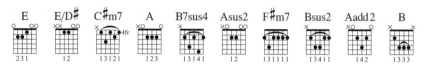

E   E/D#   C#m7   A   B7sus4   Asus2   F#m7   Bsus2   Aadd2   B

Intro

|E |E/D# |C#m7 |A |

Chorus 1

E   E/D#
  Let ev'rything that,   ev'rything that,

C#m7   A   B7sus4
  Ev'rything that has breath praise the Lord.

E   E/D#
  Let ev'rything that,   ev'rything that,

C#m7   A   B7sus4
  Ev'rything that has breath praise the Lord.

Verse 1

E   E/D#
  Praise You in the morning,   praise You in the evening,

C#m7   Asus2
  Praise You when I'm young and when I'm old.

E   E/D#
  Praise You when I'm laughing,   praise You when I'm grieving,

C#m7   Asus2
  Praise You ev'ry season of the soul.

   F#m7   Bsus2
If we could see how much You're worth,

   F#m7   Bsus2
Your pow'r, Your might, Your endless love,

   F#m7   Bsus2   Aadd2 B
Then surely we would never cease to praise.

Chorus 2   *Repeat Chorus 1*

Verse 2
```
             E                      E/D♯
             Praise You in the heavens,   joining with the angels,

             C♯m7                    Asus2
             Praising You forever and a day.

             E                      E/D♯
             Praise You on the earth now,   joining with creation,

             C♯m7                    Asus2
             Calling all the nations to your praise.

              F♯m7          Bsus2
             If they could see how much You're worth,

                F♯m7              Bsus2
             Your pow'r, Your might, Your endless love.

                F♯m7          Bsus2      Aadd2  B
             Then surely they would never cease to praise.
```

Chorus 3   *Repeat Chorus 1*
```
             | E        ‖
```

Light the Fire Again

Words and Music by
Brian Doerksen

Melody:

Don't let ___ our love ___ grow cold. ___

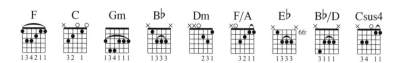

Chorus 1

    F   C
    Don't let our love ____ grow cold.

    Gm   **B♭**
    I'm calling out, "Light the fire again."

    F   C
    Don't let our vi - sion die.

    Gm   **B♭**   **F** **C** **Gm** **B♭**
    I'm calling out, "Light the fire again."

Chorus 2

    F   C
    You know my heart, ____ my deeds.

    Gm   **B♭**
    I'm calling out, "Light the fire again."

    F   C
    I need Your dis - cipline.

    Gm   **B♭**   **F**
    I'm calling out, "Light the fire again."

Verse 1

```
       Gm                      Dm                      C
       I am here to buy gold ___ refined in the fire.

         Bb                      F/A                   C
       Na - ked and poor, wretch - ed and blind I come.

                              Eb  Bb/D              Csus4
       Cloth me in white _____ so I won't be ___ ashamed.

       Bb                      F          C  Gm  Bb
       Lord, light the fire ___ again.
```

Chorus 3   *Repeat Chorus 1*

Chorus 4   *Repeat Chorus 2*

Verse 2   *Repeat Verse 1*

Outro

```
       Bb                      F          C  Gm
       Lord, light the fire ___ again.

       Bb                      F          C  Gm
       Lord, light the fire ___ again.

       Bb                      F
       Lord, light the fire ___ again.
```

Lord, Reign in Me

Words and Music by
Brenton Brown

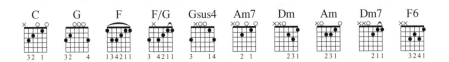

O - ver all the __ earth __ You reign on __ high. __

C   G   F   F/G   Gsus4   Am7   Dm   Am   Dm7   F6

Intro | C   G | F   F/G | C   G | F |

Verse 1

      C   G   F   Gsus4
    Over all the earth ____ You reign on high.

      C   G   F   G
    Ev'ry mountain stream, ____ ev'ry sunset sky.

      Am7   G   F   G   Dm
    But my one request, ____ Lord, my only aim

             F   G
    Is that You'd reign in me again.

Chorus 1

      C   G   F   G
    Lord reign in me. ____ Reign in Your pow'r.

      C   G   F   G
    Over all my dreams, in my darkest hour,

      Am   G   F   G   Dm
    'Cause You are the Lord ____ of all I am,

             F   G
    So won't You reign in me again?

Interlude 1	|C G |F F/G|Am7 G |F |

Verse 2

    C   G   F   Gsus4
Over ev'ry thought, ___ over ev'ry word,

    C   G   F   G
May my life reflect ___ the beauty of my Lord.

    Am7   G   F   G   Dm
'Cause You mean more to me ___ than any earthly thing,

                  F   G
So won't You reign in me again?

Chorus 2	*Repeat Chorus 1*
Interlude 2	*Repeat Interlude 1*
Verse 3	*Repeat Verse 1*
Chorus 3	*Repeat Chorus 1*
Chorus 4	*Repeat Chorus 1*

Outro

    Dm7   F   G
Won't You reign, won't You reign in me again?

    Dm7   F   G
Come and reign, Lord, won't You reign in me again?

|:C   G |F6   F/G:| *Play 4 times w/ voc. ad lib.*

|C |

Lord, I Lift Your Name on High

Words and Music by
Rick Founds

Melody:

Lord, I   lift Your Name   on ___ high. ___

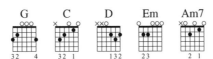

G   C   D   Em   Am7

Intro   ‖: G   C | D   C :‖

Verse 1

G   C   D   C
Lord, I lift Your name on ___ high.

G   C   D   C
Lord, I love to sing Your praises.

G   C   D   C
I'm so glad You're in my ___ life;

G   C   D
I'm so glad You came to save us.

Chorus 1

G   C   D   C
You came from heaven to earth to show the way.

G   C   D   C
From the earth ___ to the cross, my debt to pay,

G   C   D   Em
From the cross ___ to the grave, from the grave ___ to the sky.

Am7   D
Lord, I lift Your name on high.

Interlude 1	*Repeat Intro*
Verse 2	*Repeat Verse 1*
Chorus 2	*Repeat Chorus 1*
Interlude 2	*Repeat Intro*
Chorus 3	*Repeat Chorus 1*

Chorus 4

G   C   D   C
You came from heaven to earth to show the way.

G   C   D   C
From the earth ___ to the cross, my debt to pay,

G   C   D   Em
From the cross ___ to the grave, from the grave ___ to the sky.

Am7   D   C   G   C
Lord, I lift Your name on, Lord, I lift Your name on ___ high.

D   C   G
Lord, I lift Your name on ___ high.

More Precious than Silver

Words and Music by
Lynn DeShazo

Melody:

Lord,　You　are　more

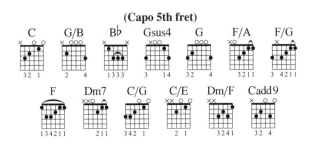

(Capo 5th fret)

C　　G/B　　B♭　　Gsus4　　G　　F/A　　F/G

F　　Dm7　　C/G　　C/E　　Dm/F　　Cadd9

Intro

| C | G/B | B♭ | Gsus4　G |

Verse 1

C　　　G/B　　F/A　　　　F/G
Lord, You are more precious than silver.

C　　　G/B　F/A　F　　Dm7　Gsus4　G
Lord, You are　　more costly　　than gold.

C　　　G/B　　F/A　　　　C/G
Lord, You are more beautiful than diamonds,

　　　Dm7　C/E　Dm/F　　Gsus4　G　C　F/G　G
And nothing I de - sire com - pares　　with You.

Verse 2

C　　　G/B　　F/A　　　　F/G　F/G
Lord, You are more precious than silver.

C　　　G/B　F/A　F　　Dm7　Gsus4　G
Lord, You are　　more costly　　than gold.

C　　　G/B　　F/A　　　　C/G
Lord, You are more beautiful than diamonds,

　　　Dm7　C/E　Dm/F　　Gsus4　G　C　　Cadd9
And nothing I de - sire com - pares　　with You.

My God Reigns

Words and Music by
Darrell Evans

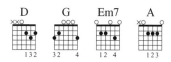

Verse 1

D   G   D
There's nowhere else that I'd rather be
   G   D   Em7   A
Than dancing with You as You sing over me.
D   G   D
There's nothing else that I'd rather do,
    Em7   D   A   D
Lord, ___than to wor - ship You.

Verse 2

Repeat Verse 1

Pre-Chorus

      D
So, re - joice, be glad, rejoice O my soul,

for the Lord, your God, He reigns forever more.
  G   D
I ___ rejoice, for my God reigns.

So, rejoice, be glad, your Father and your Friend

Is the Lord, your God, whose rule will never end.
  G
I ___ rejoice,

Chorus

       A   G   D
For my God reigns, and I dance the dance of praise.
      A   G   D
My God reigns, with a shout I will proclaim,
      A   G   D
My God reigns, and I worship without shame.
      A   G   Em7   D
My God reigns, and I will rejoice,   for my God reigns.

My Life Is in You, Lord

Words and Music by
Daniel Gardner

Melody:

My life is in You, Lord, _ my

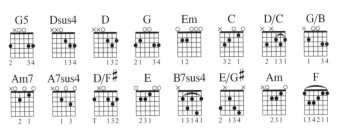

G5 Dsus4 D G Em C D/C G/B
Am7 A7sus4 D/F♯ E B7sus4 E/G♯ Am F

Intro | G5 | | | Dsus4 D |

Chorus 1
    G   Em
My life is in You, Lord, my strength is in You, Lord,
    C   G   Dsus4 D
My hope is in You, Lord, in You, it's in You.
    G   Em
My life is in You, Lord, my strength is in You, Lord,
    C   G   Dsus4 D
My hope is in You, Lord, in You, it's in You.

Verse 1
        C   D/C   G/B Am7 G
I will praise You with all of my life,
G/B C   D/C   G/B   G
I will praise You with all of my strength.
G/B D A7sus4 D/F♯ G   E B7sus4 E/G♯ Am
With all of   my   life, with all of   my   strength,
F   Am   Dsus4 D
All of my hope is in You.

Chorus 2
    G   Em
My life is in You, Lord, my strength is in You, Lord,
    C   G   Dsus4 D
My hope is in You, Lord, in You, it's in You.
    G   Em
My life is in You, Lord, my strength is in You, Lord,
    C   G   Dsus4 D G
My hope is in You, Lord, in You, it's in You,   in You.

My Redeemer Lives

Words and Music by
Reuben Morgan

I know He res-cued my soul, __

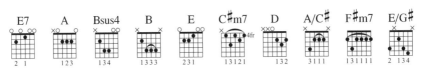

Verse 1

    E7   A   E7   A
I know He rescued my soul,   His blood has covered my sin,

    E7   A   E7 A
I believe,   I believe.

E7   A   E7   A
  My shame He's taken away,   my pain is healed in His name.

    E7   A   E7 A
I believe,   I believe.

Bsus4   B   A   B
  I'll raise a ban - ner   'cause my Lord has conquered the grave!

Chorus 1

     E   A   C♯m7   B
My Re - deemer lives!   My Re - deemer lives!

     E   A   C♯m7   B
My Re - deemer lives!   My Re - deemer lives!

Interlude |E7 |A |E7 |A |

Verse 2   *Repeat Verse 1*

Chorus 2   *Repeat Chorus 1*

Bridge

D   A/C♯
  You lift my burden   and I rise with You.

    E   F♯m7   E/G♯   B
I'm dancing on this mountain top to see Your kingdom come.

Chorus 3

     E   A   C♯m7   B
My Re - deemer lives!   My Re - deemer lives!

     E   A   C♯m7   B   E
My Re - deemer lives!   My Re - deemer lives!

Oh Lord, You're Beautiful

Words and Music by
Keith Green

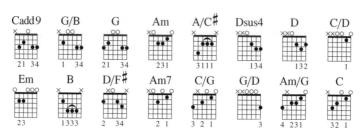

Oh, Lord,   You're beau - ti - ful.

Cadd9	G/B	G	Am	A/C#	Dsus4	D	C/D
21 34	1 34	21 34	231	3111	134	132	1

Em	B	D/F#	Am7	C/G	G/D	Am/G	C
23	1333	2 34	2 1	3 2 1	3	4 231	32 1

Intro　　　　　| Cadd9　| G/B　G　| Am　A/C# | Dsus4　D　C/D |

Verse 1

　　　　　　　G　　G/B　　　　Cadd9　G/B　D　　C/D
　　　　Oh, Lord,　　　You're beau - ti - ful.

　　　　　　　G　　G/B　Cadd9　G　D
　　　　Your face　　is all　　I seek,

　　　　　　　Em　　　　　B　　　　Em　D/F#　　G
　　　　For when Your eyes are on　this child,

　　　　G/B　Cadd9　G　D　　　　　Cadd9　　　G　　Cadd9
　　　　　Your grace　a - bounds to me.

Verse 2

　　　　　　　D　G　　G/B　　　　Cadd9　G/B　D　　C/D
　　　　Oh, Lord,　　　please light　the fire

　　　　　　　G　　G/B　　　　Cadd9　G/B　D
　　　　That once　　burned bright　and clear.

　　　　　　　Em　　　　　B　　　　Em　D/F#　G　G/B
　　　　Re-place the lamp of my　first　love

　　　　　　　Cadd9　G/B　D　　Cadd9
　　　　That burns　with holy fear.

Bridge 1

G Am7 G/B Cadd9 G/B Am C/G D/F#
I want to take   Your Word and shine it all around,

G   Am7   G/B Cadd9 A/C# G/D
But first,   help me just to live it, Lord.

D G   Am7 G/B Cadd9 G/B
And when I'm do - ing well,

Am   Am/G D/F#
Help me __ to never seek a crown,

B   Em D   C D   G   G/B
For my reward   is giving glo - ry to You.

| Cadd9 G/B | D | C/D |

Verse 3   *Repeat Verse 1*

Bridge 2

G Am7 G/B Cadd9 G/B Am C/G D/F#
I want to take   Your Word and shine it all around,

G   Am7   G/B Cadd9 A/C# G/D
But first,   help me just to live it, Lord.

D G   Am7 G/B Cadd9 G/B
And when I'm do - ing well,

Am   Am/G D/F#
Help me __ to never seek a crown,

B   Em D   C D   Cadd9
For my reward   is giving glo - ry to You.

| G/B   G | Am   A/C# | G/D   D |

Verse 4

    C/D G G/B   **Cadd9 G/B D C/D**
Oh, Lord,   You're beau - ti - ful.

    G G/B Cadd9 G/B D
Your face   is all   I   seek,

    Em   **B**   **Em D/F# G G/B**
For when Your eyes are on this child,

    Cadd9 G D   **Cadd9 G**
Your grace a - bounds to me.

C/D G G/B   **Cadd9 G/B D C/D**
 Oh, Lord,   You're beau - ti - ful.

    G G/B Cadd9 G/B D
Your face   is all   I   seek,

    Em   **B**   **Em D/F# G G/B**
For when Your eyes are on this child,

    Cadd9 G D   **Cadd9 G**
Your grace a - bounds to me.

 |**G/B G** |**Am A/C#**|**G/D D G**

Refiner's Fire

Words and Music by
Brian Doerksen

Pu - ri - fy ___ my heart, ___ let me be as

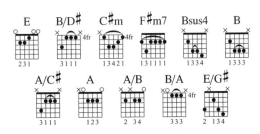

Verse 1

    E   B/D#   C#m   F#m7
Purify ___ my heart, ___ let me be as gold

      Bsus4 B   A/C# B/D#
And pre - cious sil - ver.

    E   B/D#   C#m   F#m7 E   B
Purify ___ my heart, ___ let me be as gold,   pure gold.

Chorus 1

    E   A   B   E   A   B
Re - finer's fire, ___ my heart's one desire

    A/B E B   E   A   B
Is to be holy, set apart ___ for You, ___ Lord.

     A/B   E B   B/A E/G#   A   E   B
I choose to be holy,   set apart ___ for You ___, my Mas - ter

    F#m7   B   E
Ready to do ___ Your will.

Verse 2

    E   B/D#   C#m   F#m7
Purify ___ my heart, ___ cleanse me from with - in

      Bsus4 B A/C# B/D#
And make   me ho - ly.

    E   B/D#   C#m   F#m7 E   B
Purify ___ my heart, ___ cleanse me from my sin   deep with - in.

Chorus 2   *Repeat Chorus 1*

Open the Eyes of My Heart

Words and Music by
Paul Baloche

Melody:

O - pen the eyes _ of my heart, _ Lord.

(Capo 5th fret)

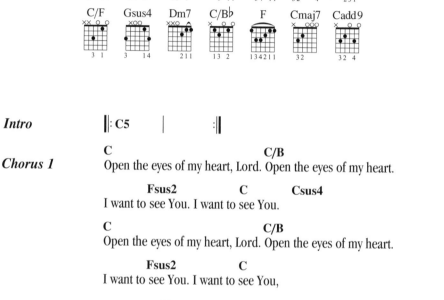

Intro	‖: C5 | :‖	

Chorus 1
    C   **C/B**
Open the eyes of my heart, Lord. Open the eyes of my heart.

            Fsus2   **C**   **Csus4**
I want to see You. I want to see You.

    C   **C/B**
Open the eyes of my heart, Lord. Open the eyes of my heart.

            Fsus2   **C**
I want to see You. I want to see You,

Verse 1
                G
To see You high and lifted up,

    Am   **C/F**   **Gsus4**
 Shin - ing in the light of Your glo - ry.

    G   **Am**   **Dm7**   **Gsus4**
Pour out Your power and love ____ as we sing holy, holy, ho - ly.

Interlude 1   \|C   \| **Csus4** \|C   \| **Csus4** \|

Chorus 2	*Repeat Chorus 1*
Verse 2	*Repeat Verse 1*
Verse 3	*Repeat Verse 1*

                    C   Cmaj7

Outro ||: (Holy, holy, holy. Holy, holy, holy.

F   C   Csus4

Holy, holy, holy, I want to see You.)   :|| *Play 3 times*

 C   Cmaj7

(Holy, holy, holy. Holy, holy, holy.

F   C

Holy, holy, holy, I want to see You.)

Fsus2   C   Fsus2   C   Fsus2   Cadd9

  I want to see You.   I want to see you.

The Potter's Hand

Words and Music by
Darlene Zschech

Melody:

Beau-ti-ful Lord, _ won-der-ful Sav - ior,

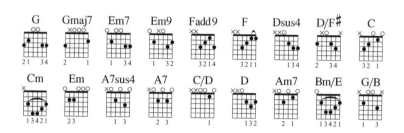

G	Gmaj7	Em7	Em9	Fadd9	F	Dsus4	D/F#	C
Cm	Em	A7sus4	A7	C/D	D	Am7	Bm/E	G/B

Intro |G   Gmaj7 |Em7   Em9 |Fadd9   F |Dsus4 |

Verse 1
G   D/F#
Beautiful Lord, wonderful Savior,

C   Cm   Em
I know for sure all of my days are held in Your hand,

A7sus4   A7   C/D   D
Crafted into ____ your perfect plan.

Verse 2
G   D/F#
You gently call me into Your presence,

C   Cm
Guiding me by Your Holy Spirit.

Em   A7sus4   A7 C/D   D
Teach me, dear Lord, to live all of my life ____ through your eyes.

Pre-Chorus 1
Em   D/F#
I'm captured by Your holy calling.

G   C   G   D/F#   Em
Set me apart; I know You're draw - ing me ____ to Yourself.

A7sus4   A7 Dsus4 D
Lead me, Lord, ____ I ____ pray.

	G D/F# Am7 Bm/E Em
Chorus 1	Take me, and mold me, use me, fill me.

     F   C   Am7 G/B Dsus4 D
I give my life to ___ the Potter's hand.

G   D/F#   Am7   Bm/E Em
Call me, guide me, lead me, walk be - side   me.

     F   C   Am7 G/B C/D
I give my life to ___ the Potter's hand.

Verse 3	*Repeat Verse 2*
Pre-Chorus 2	*Repeat Pre-Chorus 1*

	G D/F# Am7 Bm/E Em
Chorus 2	Take me, and mold me, use me, fill me.

     F   C   Am7 G/B Dsus4 D
I give my life to ___ the Potter's hand.

G   D/F#   Am7   Bm/E Em
Call me, guide me, lead me, walk be - side   me.

     F   C   Am7 G/B Dsus4 D
I give my life to ___ the Potter's hand.

Chorus 3	*Repeat Chorus 1*
Outro	‖: G Gmaj7 |Em7 Em9 |Fadd9 F |
	|Dsus4 D :‖ *Play 3 times w/ voc. ad lib.*
	|G ‖

Sanctuary

Words and Music by
John Thompson and Randy Scruggs

Melody:

Lord, pre - pare me __ to be a sanc-tu - ar - y,

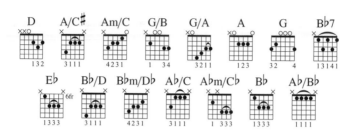

Intro |D |A/C♯ Am/C |G/B G/A A |D G/A |

Chorus 1
A   D   A
Lord, pre - pare me to be a sanctu - ary,

        G G/A   D A
Pure and holy, tried and true.

              D   A   G G/A A D G/A
With thanks - giving, I'll be a living sanctu-ary   for You.

Chorus 2
A   D   A
Lord, pre - pare me to be a sanctu - ary,

        G G/A   D A
Pure and holy, tried and true.

              D   A   G G/A A D
With thanks - giving, I'll be a living sanctu-ary   for You.

Chorus 3
B♭7   E♭   B♭/D B♭m/D♭
Lord, pre - pare me to be a sanctu - ary,

    A♭/C A♭m/C♭   E♭ B♭
Pure and holy,   tried and true.

              E♭   B♭/D B♭m/D♭ A♭/C A♭/B♭ B♭ E♭
With thanks - giving, I'll be a living   sanctu - ary   for You.

Shine on Us

Words and Music by
Michael W. Smith and Debbie Smith

Lord, _____ let Your light,

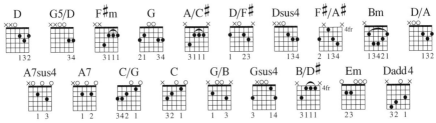

Intro

| D | | G5/D | D | | F#m |
| G | | A/C# | D | | |

Verse 1

D   G5/D   D
Lord, let Your light,

F#m   G   A/C# D
Light of Your face shine on   us.

G5/D   D
Lord, let Your light,

F#m   G   A/C# D
Light of Your face shine on   us

Chorus 1

D/F# G A/C#   D
That   we may be saved,

D/F# G A/C#   Dsus4 D
That   we may have life

D/F#   G
To find our way

F#/A#   Bm   G
In the darkest night.

D/A   A7sus4 A7
Let Your light __ shine on   us.

Interlude | D | | G5/D | D | | F#m |
| G | | A/C# | D | | |

Verse 2

D   G5/D   D
Lord, let Your grace,

    F#m   G   A/C# D
Grace from Your hand fall on   us.

    G5/D   D
Lord, let Your grace,

    F#m   G   A/C# D
Grace from Your hand fall on   us

Chorus 2

D/F# G A/C# D
That we may be saved,

D/F# G A/C#   Dsus4 D
That we may have life

   D/F#   G
To find our way

    F#/A# Bm G
In the darkest night.

          D/A   A7sus4 A7
Let Your light __ shine on   us.

Verse 3

G   C/G   G
Lord, let Your love,

   Bm   C   D/F# G
Love with no end come over us.

   C/G   G
Lord, let Your love,

   Bm   C   D/F# G
Love with no end come over us.

Chorus 3

G/B C D/F# G
That we may be saved,

G/B C D/F#   Gsus4 G
That we may have life

  G/B   C
To find our way

    B/D#   Em C
In the darkest night.

      G5/D   Dsus4 D   Em Dadd4 C
Let Your love __ come o   -   ver us.

      G5/D   Dsus4 D
Let Your light __ shine on

Outro

| G | | C/G | G | | Bm |
us.

| C | | Bm | C | | D/F# | G | ‖

Shine, Jesus, Shine

Words and Music by
Graham Kendrick

Melody:

Lord, the light of Your love is shin - ing,

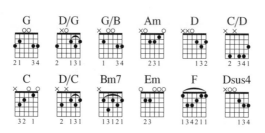

Intro

| G D/G G | G/B | Am D | G C/D D |

Verse 1

G   C   G   D
Lord, the light of Your love is shining,

G   C   G   D
In the midst of the darkness shining.

C   D/C   Bm7   Em
Jesus, Light of the world, shine up - on us,

C   D/C   Bm7   Em
Set us free by the truth You now bring us.

Chorus 1

F   Dsus4 D F   Dsus4 D
Shine on me, _____ shine on me.

G   D/G C   G/B Am   C/D D   C/D D
Shine, Jesus, shine, fill this   land with the Fa - ther's glo - ry.

G   D/G C   G/B Am Am/G F Dsus4 D
Blaze, Spirit, blaze, set our   hearts on   fire.

G   D/G C   G/B Am   C/D D C/D D
Flow, river, flow, flood the   nations with grace and mer - cy.

G   D/G   C   G/B Am D   G C/D D
Send forth Your Word, Lord, and let   there be light.

GUITAR CHORD SONGBOOK

Verse 2

G   C   G   D
Lord, I come to Your awesome presence,

G   C   G   D
From the shadows in - to Your radiance.

C   D/C   Bm7   Em
By the blood I may enter Your brightness.

C   D/C   Bm7   Em
Search me, try me, con - sume all my darkness.

Chorus 2

Repeat Chorus 1

Verse 3

G   C   G   D
As we gaze on Your Kingly brightness,

G   C   G   D
So our faces dis - play Your likeness.

C   D/C   Bm7   Em
Ever changing from glory to glory,

C   D/C   Bm7   Em
Mirrored here may our lives tell Your story.

Chorus 3

G   C   G   D
As we gaze on Your Kingly brightness,

G   C   G   D
So our faces dis - play Your likeness.

C   D/C   Bm7   Em
Ever changing from glory to glory,

C   D/C   Bm7   Em
Mirrored here may our lives tell Your story.

Shout to the Lord

Words and Music by
Darlene Zschech

Melody:

My Je - sus,   my Sav - ior,

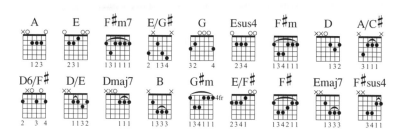

Intro | A | E   F#m7 E/G# | A | G   Esus4 E |

Verse 1
     A   E   F#m   E   D
    My Jesus,   my Savior, Lord, there is none ____ like You.

          A/C#   D   A
  All of my days   I want to praise

    F#m7   G   D6/F# Esus4 E D/E
  The wonders of Your might - y   love.

  A   E   F#m   E   D
    My comfort,   my shelter, Tower of ref - uge and strength,

        A/C#   D   A
  Let ev'ry breath, all that I am,

  F#m   G   D6/F# Esus4 E
  Never cease to wor - ship   You.

Chorus 1

A   F#m   D   D/E E
Shout to the Lord, ____ all the earth, ____ let us sing;

A   F#m   Dmaj7   Esus4 E
Power and maj - esty, praise ____ to the King!

F#m   E   D
Mountains bow down and the seas ____ will roar

    E F#m E/G#
At the sound of Your name.

A   F#m   D   D/E E
I sing for joy ____ at the work ____ of Your hands,

 A   F#m   Dmaj7   Esus4 E
For - ever I'll love ____ You, forev - er I'll stand.

F#m   E   D
Nothing compares to the prom - ise

   D/E E A E F#m7 E/G#
I have ____ in You.

Verse 2   *Repeat Verse 1*

Chorus 2

A   F#m   D   D/E E
Shout to the Lord, ____ all the earth, ____ let us sing;

A   F#m   Dmaj7   Esus4 E
Power and maj - esty, praise ____ to the King!

F#m   E   D
Mountains bow down and the seas ____ will roar

    E F#m E/G#
At the sound of Your name.

B   G#m   E   E/F# F#
I sing for joy ____ at the work ____ of Your hands,

 B   G#m   Emaj7 F#sus4 F#
For - ever I'll love ____ You, forev - er I'll stand.

G#m   F# E E/F# F#
Nothing compares to the prom - ise I have in,

B   G#m   E   E/F# F#
Nothing compares ____ to the prom - ise I have in,

B   G#m   E   E/F# F# B
Nothing compares ____ to the prom - ise I have in You.

Shout to the North

Words and Music by
Martin Smith

Men of faith, rise up and sing of the

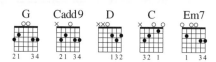

Intro ‖: G | Cadd9 :‖ *Play 3 times*
|G | |

Verse 1
G   D   Cadd9   G   D   Cadd9
Men of faith, rise up and sing of the great and glorious King.

G   D   Cadd9   G   D   Cadd9
You are strong when you feel weak; in your broken - ness, com - plete.

Chorus 1
G   C   D   G   C   D
Shout to the north and the south; sing to the east and the west.

G   C   D C   D   G
Jesus is Savior to all, Lord of heaven and earth.

Verse 2
G   D   Cadd9   G   D   Cadd9
Rise up woman of the truth; stand and sing to broken hearts.

G   D   Cadd9   G   D   Cadd9
Who can know the healing pow'r of our awesome King of love?

Chorus 2 *Repeat Chorus 1*

Chorus 3

        G   C   D   G   C   D
We will shout to the north and the south, sing to the east and the west.

Em7 C   D C   D   G
Jesus is Savior of all, Lord of heaven and earth.

Bridge

Em7   Cadd9
We've been through fire, we've been through rain,

Em7   Cadd9
We've been refined by the pow'r of His name.

Em7   Cadd9
We've fallen deeper in love with You;

                  D
You've burned the truth on our lips.

Chorus 4

        G   N.C.
We will shout to the north and the south; sing to the east and the west.

Jesus is Savior to all, Lord of heaven and earth.

Chorus 5   *Repeat Chorus 3*

Verse 3

        G   D   Cadd9   G   D   Cadd9
Rise up, church, with broken wings; fill this place with songs a - gain,

      G   D   Cadd9   G   D   Cadd9
Of our God who reigns on high. By His grace, a - gain we'll fly.

Chorus 6   *Repeat Chorus 1*

Chorus 7   *Repeat Chorus 3*

Outro

        C   D   G   C   D   G
Oh, Lord of heaven and earth. Oh, Lord of heaven and earth.

        C   D   G
Oh, Lord of heaven and earth.

So Good to Me

Words and Music by
Darrell Evans and Matt Jones

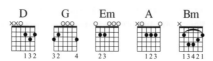

D   G   Em   A   Bm

Verse 1

        D   G Em   A   D G Em A
Oh, God, ____   You've been so good to me.

        D   G
You came and found this orphan

        Em   A   D   G Em A
And You brought me right in - to Your family.

        D   G Em   A   D G Em A
Oh, God, ____   You've been so good to me.

        D   G
You threw away my past

        Em   A   D
And You never count my sins against ___ me.

G Em   A G Em D
Oh, ___ thank You, Lord.

Pre-Chorus 1

N.C.   G Em D
  You got me dancing,

N.C.   G Em D
  And now I'm shouting.

N.C.   G Em
  You got me leaping,

        G
and now I'm spinning. Hallelujah!

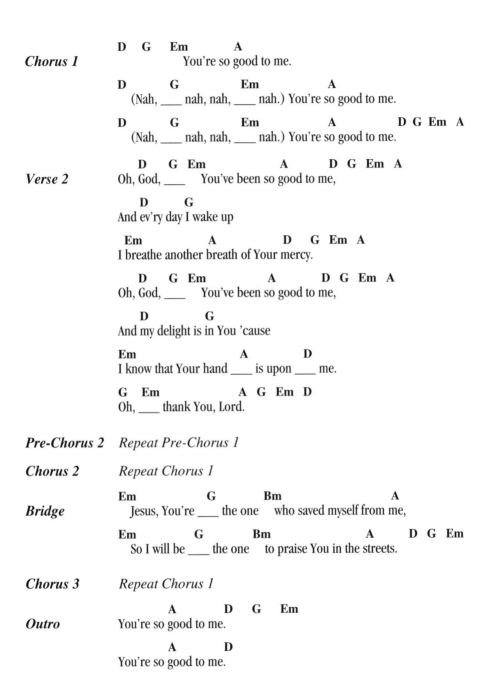

Chorus 1

D G Em A
You're so good to me.

D G   Em   A
(Nah, ___ nah, nah, ___ nah.) You're so good to me.

D G   Em   A   D G Em A
(Nah, ___ nah, nah, ___ nah.) You're so good to me.

Verse 2

D G Em   A D G Em A
Oh, God, ___ You've been so good to me,

D G
And ev'ry day I wake up

Em   A   D G Em A
I breathe another breath of Your mercy.

D G Em   A D G Em A
Oh, God, ___ You've been so good to me,

D G
And my delight is in You 'cause

Em   A   D
I know that Your hand ___ is upon ___ me.

G Em   A G Em D
Oh, ___ thank You, Lord.

Pre-Chorus 2 *Repeat Pre-Chorus 1*

Chorus 2 *Repeat Chorus 1*

Bridge

Em   G Bm   A
Jesus, You're ___ the one who saved myself from me,

Em   G Bm   A D G Em
So I will be ___ the one to praise You in the streets.

Chorus 3 *Repeat Chorus 1*

Outro

A D G Em
You're so good to me.

A D
You're so good to me.

Step by Step

Words and Music by
David Strasser "Beaker"

Melody:

Oh, God, You are my __ God,

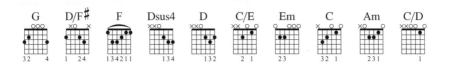

G D/F# F Dsus4 D C/E Em C Am C/D

Intro | G | D/F# | F | Dsus4 D |

Verse 1

      G   D/F# D
Oh, God, You are my God,

      C/E D   G Dsus4
And I will ever praise You.

D G   D/F# D
Oh, God, You are my God,

      C/E D   G
And I will ever praise You.

Chorus 1

       Em   Dsus4 D
I will seek You in the morn - ing,

            C   Am C/D
And I will learn to walk in Your ways.

      G   D/F# D
And step by step You'll lead ____ me,

      C/E   D   G   C/E D
And I will follow You all of my days.

Verse 2   *Repeat Verse 1*

Chorus 2

         Em   **Dsus4** **D**
I will seek You in the morn - ing,

             C   **Am** **C/D**
And I will learn to walk in Your ways.

   G   **D/F#**   **D**
And step by step You'll lead ___ me,

        C/E   **D**   **G**
And I will follow You all of my days.

         Em   **Dsus4** **D**
And I will follow You all of my days,

             C   **F** **C/D**
And I will follow You all of my days.

   G   **D**
And step by step You'll lead ___ me,

        C/E   **D**   **G**
And I will follow You all of my days.

There Is a Redeemer

Words and Music by
Melody Green

Melody:

G   Am7   G/B   C   D7   C/D   D

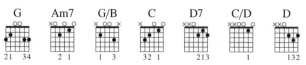

21 34   2 1   1 3   32 1   2 1 3   1   1 3 2

Intro
|G   Am7 G/B|C   G/B |Am7 D7 |G   C/D D |

Verse 1

G   D G C   G
There is a re-deem-er,

Am7 G/B C   D   G   D
Je - sus, God's own Son.

G   Am7 G/B C   G/B
Precious Lamb of God, Mes-siah,

Am7   D7   G   C/D D
Ho - ly One.

Verse 2

G   D G C   G
Jesus, my re-deem-er,

Am7 G/B C   D   G   D
Name a - bove all names.

G   Am7 G/B C   G/B
Precious Lamb of God, Mes-siah,

Am7   D7   G   C D
Oh for sinners slain.

Chorus 1

G   G/B C G
Thank You, oh my Fa-ther,

C   G   D7
For giving us Your Son,

G   Am7 G/B C
And leav-ing Your spirit

G/B   Am7   D7   G   C/D D
Till the work on earth is done.

GUITAR CHORD SONGBOOK

Verse 3

G   D   G C G
When I stand in glo-ry,

Am7 G/B C D G D
I   will see His face,

G   Am7 G/B C   G/B
And there I'll serve my King for-ever

Am7 D7 G   C D
In that holy place.

Chorus 2

G   G/B C G
Thank You, oh my Fa-ther,

C   G D7
For giving us Your Son,

G Am7 G/B C
And leav-ing Your spirit

G/B Am7   D7   G C/D D
Till the work on earth is done.

Verse 4

Repeat Verse 1

Chorus 3

G   G/B C G
Thank You, oh my Fa-ther,

C   G D7
For giving us Your Son,

G Am7 G/B C
And leav-ing Your spirit

G/B Am7   D7   G C/D D
Till the work on earth is done.

G Am7 G/B C   G/B
And leav-ing Your spirit till the

Am7   D7   G D G C G
Work on earth is done.

This Is the Day

By Les Garrett

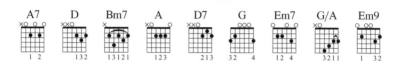

A7   D   Bm7   A   D7   G   Em7   G/A   Em9

Intro | A7 | | | D | |

Chorus

D
This is the day, this is the day

Bm7   **D**   **A**
That the Lord has made, that the Lord has made.

A7
I will rejoice, I will rejoice

      D   **D7**
And be glad in it, and be glad in it.

G   **D**   **Bm7**
This is the day that the Lord has made,

G   **D**   **Em7** **G/A**
I will re - joice and be glad in it.

D
This is the day, this is the day

Bm7   **Em9** **A7** **D**
That the Lord   has   made.

We Fall Down

Words and Music by
Chris Tomlin

Melody:

We fall __ down, __ we lay our __ crowns __

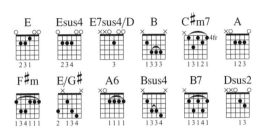

E   Esus4   E7sus4/D   B   C#m7   A
F#m   E/G#   A6   Bsus4   B7   Dsus2

Intro

| E   Esus4 | E   E7sus4/D |

Verse 1

E   B   C#m7   A   F#m
We fall down, we lay our crowns at the feet ___ of Je - sus,

E   B   C#m7   A   B
The greatness of mercy and love at the feet ___ of Je - sus.

E/G#   A6   E/G#   F#m
And we cry, "Holy, ho - ly, ho - ly,"

E/G#   A6   E/G#   F#m
And we cry, "Holy, ho - ly, ho - ly,"

C#m7 B A6   E/G#   F#m Bsus4 B7
And we   cry, "Holy, ho - ly, ho - ly   is   the Lamb."

Interlude

| E   A | E   Dsus2 |

Verse 2

Repeat Verse 1

Outro

A6   E/G#   F#m Bsus4 B7   E A E Dsus2 E
Holy, ho - ly, ho - ly   is   the Lamb.

Trading My Sorrows

Words and Music by
Darrell Evans

Melody:

I'm trad - ing __ my sor - rows, __

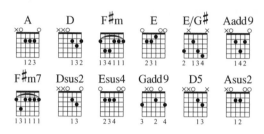

Intro
| A   D | F#m E | A   D | F#m E/G# |
| Aadd9 D | F#m E | Aadd9 D | F#m E |

Chorus 1

Aadd9   D   F#m E   Aadd9   D   F#m7 E
I'm   trading my sor - rows, I'm   trading my ___ shame;

Aadd9   D   F#m E   A Dsus2 F#m7 E
I'm   laying them down for the joy of the Lord.

Aadd9   D   F#m   E   Aadd9   D   F#m E
I'm   trading my ___ sick - ness, I'm   trading my ___ pain;

Aadd9   D   F#m   E   A Dsus2   F#m E
I'm   laying them down for the joy of the Lord.

Verse 1

           A   D   F#m   E
We say yes, Lord,   yes Lord, yes, yes, ___ Lord,

A   D   F#m   E/G#
Yes, Lord, ___ yes, Lord, yes, yes, ___ Lord,

A   D   F#m   E   A D F#m E
Yes, Lord, ___ yes, Lord, Yes, yes, ___ Lord, Amen.

Verse 2

               A   D   F#m   E
I am pressed __ but not ___ crushed; perse - cuted, not abandoned,

A   D   F#m   E/G#
    Struck down but not destroyed.

            A   D   F#m   E
I am blessed ___ beyond the curse, for His promise will endure,

         A   D   F#m   E
That His joy is gonna be my strength.

                  Esus4   E
Though the sorrow may last for the night,

          Gadd9   D5
His joy ___ comes with the morn - ing.

Chorus 2   *Repeat Chorus 1*

Verse 3   *Repeat Verse 1*

Verse 4   *Repeat Verse 1*

Verse 5   *Repeat Verse 2*

Chorus 3   *Repeat Chorus 1*

Interlude   ‖:Asus2 D5 │F#m   E   │Asus2 D5   │F#m   E   :‖

Bridge
          Aadd9   D5   F#m   E
‖: La, la, la,   la; la, la, la, la, la, la, la,

        Aadd9   D5   F#m   E/G#
La, la, la,   la, la, la, la, la, la,   la, la,

        Aadd9   D5   F#m   E   Aadd9   D5   F#m   E
La, la, la,   la, la, la, la, la, la, la, la, la, la.   :‖

│Aadd9   Dsus2 │F#m   E   │

                   A   Dsus2   F#m7   E/G#
Time to run and play with the Lord now,

            A   Dsus2   F#m   E
Set my feet a dancin',   put a new song in my heart.

│Aadd9   Dsus2 │F#m   E   │

Outro   *Repeat Chorus 1 and fade*

We Bow Down

Words and Music by
Twila Paris

Melody:

You are _ Lord of cre-a - tion

Chord diagrams: C, Csus4, G/C, F/G, G/B, Am, Dm/F, G7, G7sus4/F, C/E, G, F

Intro

| C | | Csus4 | | C | | Csus4 | |
| C | | Csus4 | | C | | Csus4 | |

Verse 1

        C   **G/C** **C**
You are Lord of creation and Lord of my life,

              G/C
Lord of the land and the sea.

F/G **C**   **G/B**   **Am**
You were Lord of the heavens be - fore there was time,

Dm/F   **F/G** **G7** **C**
And Lord of all lords ___ You will be.

Chorus 1

   G7sus4/F **C/E**   **G**   **C**
We bow down _____ and we worship You, Lord.

   G7sus4/F **C/E**   **G**   **C**
We bow down _____ and we worship You, Lord.

   G7sus4/F **C/E**   **G**   **Am**
We bow down _____ and we worship You, Lord.

Dm/F   **G**   **G7** **C** **Csus4** **C** **Csus4**
Lord of all lords ___ You will be.

Verse 2

        C   **G/C** **C**
You are King of creation and King of my life,

              G/C
King of the land and the sea.

F/G **C**   **G/B**   **Am**
You were King of the heavens be - fore there was time,

Dm/F   **F/G** **G7** **C**
And King of all kings ___ You will be.

Chorus 2

        G7sus4/F   C/E   G   C
We bow down _____ and we crown You the King.

        G7sus4/F   C/E   G   C
We bow down _____ and we crown You the King.

        G7sus4/F   C/E   G   Am
We bow down _____ and we crown You the King.

Dm/F   G   G7
King of all kings ____ You will

Interlude

C				

Be.

G/C	C			

G/C		F/G	C		

G/B	Am	F		F/G	G

G/C		

Chorus 3

        G7sus4/F   C/E   G   C
We bow down _____ and we worship You, Lord.

        G7sus4/F   C/E   G   C
We bow down _____ and we worship You, Lord.

        G7sus4/F   C/E   G   Am
We bow down _____ and we worship You, Lord.

Dm/F   G   G7 C
Lord of all lords ____ You will be.

Chorus 4

Repeat Chorus 2

Outro

C	Csus4	C	Csus4	

Be.

C	Csus4	C	G	Csus4

We Want to See Jesus Lifted High

Words and Music by
Doug Horley

Melody:

We want to see Je - sus lift - ed high _

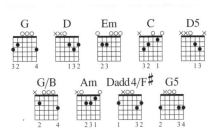

Intro   ‖: G |D |Em |C   :‖

Verse 1

  G   D
We want to see Jesus lifted high,

  Em   C
A banner that flies across this land

  G   D
That all men might see the truth and know

  Em   C
He is the way to heaven.

  G   D
We want to see Jesus lifted high,

  Em   C
A banner that flies across this land

  G   D
That all men might see the truth and know

  Em   C
He is the way to heaven.

Chorus 1

G   D5
We want to see,   we want to see,

Em   C
We want to see Je - sus lifted high.

G   D5
We want to see,   we want to see,

Em   C   G   D
We want to see Je - sus lifted high.

Verse 2   *Repeat Verse 1*

Chorus 2

G   D5
We want to see,   we want to see,

Em   C
We want to see Je - sus lifted high.

G   D5
We want to see,   we want to see,

Em   C   G
We want to see Je - sus lifted high.

Bridge

N.C.   D   Em   D   Em
Step by step we're moving for - ward; little by little talking ground,

D   Em
Ev'ry prayer ____ a powerful wea - pon.

C   D
Strongholds come tumbling down ____ and down and down and down.

Verse 3   *Repeat Verse 1 (Instrumental)*

Chorus 3   *Repeat Chorus 1 (Instrumental)*

Chorus 4

N.C.
‖: We want to see, we want to see,

We want to see Jesus lifted high.   :‖ *Play 4 times*

G   D5
‖:   We want to see,   we want to see,

Em   C
We want to see Je - sus lifted high.   :‖ *Play 4 times*

Outro/Guitar Solo   ‖: G | D | Em | C   :‖ *Play 3 times*
                  | C   G/B   Am   Dadd4/F♯ | G5   ‖

We Will Glorify

Words and Music by
Twila Paris

Melody:

We will glo-ri-fy the King of kings;

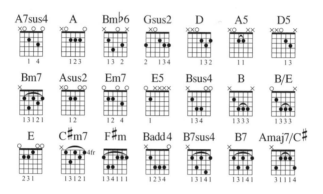

A7sus4 A Bm♭6 Gsus2 D A5 D5
Bm7 Asus2 Em7 E5 Bsus4 B B/E
E C#m7 F#m Badd4 B7sus4 B7 Amaj7/C#

Intro

A7sus4		A	Bm♭6 A7sus4	Gsus2
A7sus4		A	Bm♭6 A7sus4	D

Verse 1

     A5   D5   A5   D5
We will glorify the King of kings; we will glorify the Lamb.

     A5   Bm7   Asus4   D5
We will glorify the Lord of lords, who is the great I Am.

    Asus2   D5   Asus4   D5
Lord Je - hovah reigns in majesty; we will bow before His throne.

    Asus2   Bm7   Em7 A7sus4 D
We will worship Him in righteousness; we will worship Him a - lone.

  A7sus4 D5   A7sus4   D5
We will glorify the King of kings; we will glorify the Lamb.

  A7sus4 Bm♭6   Em7 A7sus4   D
We will glorify the Lord of lords, who is the great I   Am.

GUITAR CHORD SONGBOOK

Interlude | A7sus4 | A | Bm♭6 A7sus4 | D |

E5   Bsus4 B   B/E   E   Bsus4 B   E
Verse 2   He is Lord of heaven, Lord of earth; He is Lord of all who live.

   Bsus4 B   C#m7   F#m   Bsus4 B E
He is Lord of all the universe; all praise to Him   we give.

        Bsus4 B   B/E   E   Bsus4 B   E
Oh, halle - lujah   to the King of kings, halle - lujah   to the Lamb.

        Bsus4 B   C#m7   F#m Bsus4   B E
Halle - lujah   to the Lord of lords, who is the great   I Am.

     Badd4   B/E   E   Badd4   E
We will glorify the King of kings; we will glorify the Lamb.

     Badd4   C#m7   F#m   Bsus4 C#m7
We will glorify the Lord of lords, who is the   great I Am.

      F#m   B7sus4 E5   B7sus4   B7   Amaj7/C#   B7sus4 E
Who is the   great I   Am.

Worthy, You Are Worthy

Words and Music by
Don Moen

Melody:

Wor - thy,   You are wor - thy,

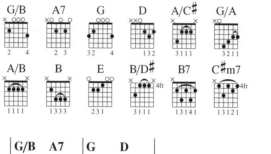

G/B   A7   G   D   A/C#   G/A

A/B   B   E   B/D#   B7   C#m7

Intro
| G/B   A7 | G   D |

Chorus 1

D   A/C#
Worthy, You are worthy,

    G/B   A7   G   D   G/A
King of kings, Lord of lords, You are wor - thy.

D   A/C#
Worthy, You are worthy,

    G/B   A7   D   G/A
King of kings, Lord of lords, I worship You.

Chorus 2

    D   A/C#
Holy, You are holy,

    G/B   A7   G   D   G/A
King of kings, Lord of lords, You are ho - ly.

D   A/C#
Holy, You are holy,

    G/B   A7   D   A/B   B
King of kings, Lord of lords, I worship You.

Chorus 3

E   B/D#
Jesus, You are Jesus.

    A/C#   B7   A   E   A/B
King of kings, Lord of lords, You are Je - sus.

E   B/D#   A/C#   B7   E
Jesus, You are Jesus. King of kings, Lord of lords, I worship You.

C#m7   A   B   B7   A   E
King of kings, Lord of lords, I worship You.

You Are So Good to Me

Words and Music by Don Chaffer,
Ben Pasley and Robin Pasley

Well, You are beau - ti - ful — my sweet, sweet —

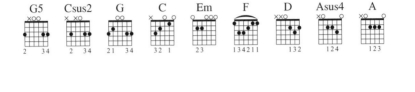

		G5		Csus2

Intro

                  G5   **Csus2**
Well, You are beautiful my sweet, sweet song.

     G5   **Csus2**
You are beautiful my sweet, sweet song.

            G   **Csus2**
Well, You are beautiful my sweet, sweet song ____ and I will sing again.

Interlude 1 | G5 | C | G5 | C |

Verse 1

          G   **Csus2**
You are so good to me. You heal my broken heart.

          G   **Csus2**
You are my Father in Heav - en.

          G   **Csus2**
You are so good to me. You heal my broken heart.

          G   **Csus2**
You are my Father in Heav - en.

             G5   **Csus2**
Well, you are beautiful my sweet, sweet song.

             Em   **Csus2**
You are beautiful my sweet, sweet song.

	G Csus2
Verse 2	You ride upon the clouds. You lead me to the truth.

            G   Csus2
You are the Spirit inside ____ me.

            G   Csus2
You ride upon the clouds. You lead me to the truth.

            G   Csus2
You are the Spirit inside ____ me.

                G5   Csus2
Well, you are beautiful my sweet, sweet song.

                Em   Csus2
You are beautiful my sweet, sweet song.

                G5   Csus2
You are beautiful my sweet, sweet song ____ and I will sing again.

Interlude 2 | F | C | F | C |

              D   C   G
Bridge   You are my strong melody, yeah.

              D   C   G
                You are my dancing rhythm.

              D   C   G
                You are my perfect rhyme

                      Em   Asus4   A
              And I will sing of You for - ever.

Verse 3

    G   C
You poured out all Your blood. You died upon the cross.

    G   C
You are my Jesus who loves ___ me.

    G   C
You poured out all Your blood. You died upon the cross.

    G   C
You are my Jesus who loves ___ me.

      G5   Csus2
You are beautiful my sweet, sweet song.

      Em   Csus2
You are beautiful my sweet, sweet song.

      G5   Csus2
You are beautiful my sweet, sweet song ___ and I will sing again.

Outro

      G5
‖: You are beautiful my sweet, sweet song

Csus2
  And I will sing again. :‖ *Play 3 times*

      G5
You are beautiful my sweet, sweet song.

Csus2 G5   C
  You   are my Father in Heav - en.

           G   C
Well, You are the Spirit inside ___ me.

    G   C
You are my Jesus who loves ____ me.

You Alone

Words and Music by
Jack Parker and David Crowder

Melody:

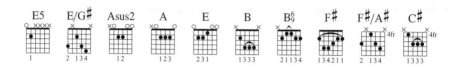

You ___ are   the on - ly ___ one

E5   E/G#   Asus2   A   E   B   B♭9/6   F#   F#/A#   C#

Intro

‖: E5   E/G# | Asus2   :‖

Verse 1

E   E/G# Asus2 A   E
You are the only   one I need.

E/G# Asus2 A   E
I bow all of me at Your feet.

E/G# Asus2   A   E5 E/G# Asus2
I   worship You a - lone.

Verse 2

E   E/G# Asus2   A
You have   given me more

      E E/G# Asus2   A
Than I   could   ever have wanted,

      E E/G# Asus2   A   E5 E/G# Asus2
And I   want to give You my heart and my soul.

Chorus 1

E   E/G#   A
You ___ alone ___ are Father,

      E E/G#   A   B
And You _____ alone ___ are good.

E   E/G#   A
You ___ alone ___ are Savior,

      E E/G#   A
And You _____ alone ___ are God.

Interlude	*Repeat Intro*
Verse 3	*Repeat Verse 1*
Verse 4	*Repeat Verse 2*

Chorus 2

E   E/G#   A
You ___ alone ___ are Father,

       E EG#   A   B
And You _____ alone ___ are good.

E   E/G#   A
You ___ alone ___ are Savior,

       E E/G#   A   B⁶/₉
And You _____ alone ___ are God.

Bridge

  F#   F#/A#   B
‖: I'm alive, ___ I'm alive, ___ I'm alive, I'm alive.

F#   F#/A#   B
 I'm alive, ___ I'm alive, ___ I'm alive, I'm alive. :‖

Chorus 3

F# F#/A#   B
You ___ alone ___ are Father,

       F# F#/A#   B   C#
And You _____ alone ___ are good.

F# F#/A#   B
You ___ alone ___ are Savior,

       F# F#/A#   B   C#
And You _____ alone ___ are God.

Chorus 4   *Repeat Chorus 3*

| F#   ‖

You Are My King

(Amazing Love)

Words and Music by
Billy James Foote

Melody:

I'm for-giv - en ____ be-cause You were _

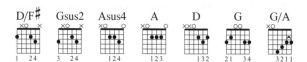

D/F#   Gsus2   Asus4   A   D   G   G/A

Intro

| D/F# Gsus2 | Asus4 | D/F# Gsus2 | Asus4   A |

Verse 1

D/F#   Gsus2 Asus4   A
I'm forgiv - en be - cause You were forsak - en.

D/F#   Gsus2 Asus2   A
I'm ac - cepted;   You were con - demned.

D/F#   Gsus2   Asus4   A
I'm alive ____ and well; Your Spirit is within ____ me

    Gsus2   A   D
Be - cause You died ____ and rose again.

Verse 2

Repeat Verse 1

Chorus 1

D   G
Amazing love, how ____ can it be

D   Asus4   A   G/A
That You, my King, would die for me?

D   G
Amazing love, I ____ know it's true;

D   Asus4   A
It's my joy to honor You.

      G   A   D
In all I ____ do,   I honor You.

Verse 3	*Repeat Verse 1*
Chorus 2	*Repeat Chorus 1*

Bridge

D
You are my King. You are my King.

Jesus, You are my King. Jesus, You are my King.

Chorus 3   *Repeat Chorus 1*

Ouotro

        G   **A**   **D**
In all I ___ do, I honor You.

Guitar Chord Songbooks

Each book includes complete lyrics, chord symbols, and guitar chord diagrams.

Acoustic Rock

A handy collection of 80 acoustic favorites: Angie • Blackbird • Blowin' in the Wind • Bridge over Troubled Water • Drive • Dust in the Wind • Fast Car • Here Comes the Sun • If You Could Only See • Layla • Maggie May • Me and Julio down by the Schoolyard • Mrs. Robinson • Pink Houses • The Sound of Silence • Torn • Yesterday • and more.
00699540 . . . .$17.95

The Beatles (A-I)

An awesome reference of Beatles hits: All You Need Is Love • And I Love Her • The Ballad of John and Yoko • Blackbird • Can't Buy Me Love • A Day in the Life • Eight Days a Week • Eleanor Rigby • Get Back • Good Day Sunshine • A Hard Day's Night • Help! • Here Comes the Sun • Hey Jude • I Saw Her Standing There • In My Life • and more!
00699558 . . . .$16.95

The Beatles (J-Y)

100 more Beatles hits: Lady Madonna • Let It Be • Love Me Do • Michelle • Norwegian Wood • Ob-La-Di, Ob-La-Da • Paperback Writer • Revolution • Sgt. Pepper's Lonely Hearts Club Band • Strawberry Fields Forever • Twist and Shout • We Can Work It Out • When I'm Sixty-Four • Yellow Submarine • Yesterday • and more.
00699562 . . . .$16.95

The Beach Boys

59 favorites: Barbara Ann • Be True to Your School • California Girls • Catch a Wave • Don't Worry Baby • Fun, Fun, Fun • Good Vibrations • Help Me Rhonda • I Get Around • In My Room • Kokomo • Little Deuce Coupe • Surfin' U.S.A. • Wild Honey • Wouldn't It Be Nice • dozens more!
00699566 . . . .$14.95

Children's Songs

70 songs for kids: Alphabet Song • The Bear Went over the Mountain • Bingo • The Candy Man • Eensy Weensy Spider • It's a Small World • Mickey Mouse March • Old MacDonald • On Top of Spaghetti • Puff the Magic Dragon • Super-califragilisticexpialidocious • Twinkle, Twinkle Little Star • Won't You Be My Neighbor? (It's a Beautiful Day in This Neighborhood) • and more!
00699539 . . . .$12.95

Christmas Carols

80 Christmas carols: Angels We Have Heard on High • Away in a Manger • Coventry Carol • Deck the Hall • Fum, Fum, Fum • Good King Wenceslas • The Holly and the Ivy • I Saw Three Ships • Joy to the World • O Holy Night • Silent Night • Up on the Housetop • We Wish You a Merry Christmas • What Child Is This? • and more.
00699536 . . . .$12.95

Johnny Cash

58 Cash classics: A Boy Named Sue • Cry, Cry, Cry • Daddy Sang Bass • Folsom Prison Blues • I Walk the Line • The Long Black Veil • The Man in Black • Orange Blossom Special • (Ghost) Riders in the Sky • Ring of Fire • Solitary Man • Tennessee Flat Top Box • You Win Again • and more.
00699648 . . . .$14.95

Christmas Songs

80 Christmas favorites: The Christmas Song • Feliz Navidad • Grandma Got Run over by a Reindeer • I Heard the Bells on Christmas Day • Jingle-Bell Rock • Merry Christmas, Darling • Rudolph the Red-Nosed Reindeer • Silver Bells • We Need a Little Christmas • more.
00699537 . . . .$12.95

Eric Clapton

75 of Slowhand's finest: Born Under a Bad Sign • Change the World • Have You Ever Loved a Woman • I Shot the Sheriff • Knockin' on Heaven's Door • Layla • Riding with the King • Strange Brew • Tears in Heaven • Wonderful Tonight • and more!
00699567 . . . .$14.95

Classic Rock

80 rock essentials: Beast of Burden • Cat Scratch Fever • Free Ride • Hot Blooded • Layla • Money • Owner of a Lonely Heart • Rhiannon • Start Me Up • Sweet Emotion • Take Me to the River • Walk on the Wild Side • and more
00699598 . . . .$12.95

Contemporary Christian

80 hits from today's top CCM artists: Awesome God • Don't Look at Me • El Shaddai • Friends • The Great Divide • His Strength Is Perfect • I Will Be Here • Just One • Live Out Loud • A Maze of Grace • Oh Lord, You're Beautiful • Run to You • Speechless • Testify to Love • Via Dolorosa • more.
00699564 . . . .$14.95

Country

80 country standards: Always on My Mind • Boot Scootin' Boogie • Crazy • Elvira • Folsom Prison Blues • Hey, Good Lookin' • I Feel Lucky • Okie from Muskogee • Ring of Fire • Sixteen Tons • Through the Years • Your Cheatin' Heart • more.
00699534 . . . .$14.95

Cowboy Songs

Over 60 tunes: Back in the Saddle Again • Git Along, Little Dogies • Happy Trails • Home on the Range • Mexicali Rose • The Red River Valley • Sioux City Sue • Streets of Laredo • The Yellow Rose of Texas • and more.
00699636 . . . .$12.95

Folk Pop Rock

80 songs: American Pie • Constant Craving • Dust in the Wind • Here Comes the Sun • Me and Bobby McGee • Nights in White Satin • Somebody to Love • Time in a Bottle • Vincent (Starry Starry Night) • You Were Meant for Me • and more.
00699651 . . . .$12.95

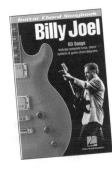
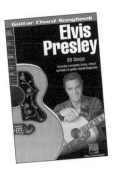
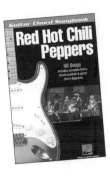

Folksongs

80 folk favorites: Aura Lee • Camptown Races • Danny Boy • Git Along, Little Dogies • Home on the Range • I've Been Working on the Railroad • Man of Constant Sorrow • Matilda • Nobody Knows the Trouble I've Seen • Scarborough Fair • When the Saints Go Marching In • and more.
00699541 . . . .$12.95

Billy Joel

60 Billy Joel favorites: Allentown • Honesty • It's Still Rock and Roll to Me • Just the Way You Are • Keeping the Faith • The Longest Time • My Life • New York State of Mind • Piano Man • Pressure • She's Always a Woman • Uptown Girl • We Didn't Start the Fire • You May Be Right • and more.
00699632 . . . .$14.95

Pop/Rock

80 chart hits: Against All Odds • All I Wanna Do • Closer to Free • Come Sail Away • Every Breath You Take • Give Me One Reason • Heartache Tonight • Hurts So Good • Imagine • Kokomo • Let It Be • More Than Words • Smooth • So Far Away • Summer of '69 • Twist and Shout • What I Like About You • Wonderful Tonight • and more.
00699538 . . . .$14.95

Elvis Presley

60 hits from The King: All Shook Up • Blue Suede Shoes • Can't Help Falling in Love • Don't Be Cruel (To a Heart That's True) • Heartbreak Hotel • Hound Dog • It's Now or Never • Jailhouse Rock • Love Me Tender • Return to Sender • Suspicious Minds • That's All Right • Viva Las Vegas • more.
00699633 . . . .$14.95

Red Hot Chili Peppers

50 hits from the Chili Peppers: Blood Sugar Sex Magik • Breaking the Girl • By the Way • Californication • Can't Stop • Get on Top • Give It Away • Higher Ground • Knock Me Down • Love Rollercoaster • One Hot Minute • Out in L.A. • Save the Population • Scar Tissue • Suck My Kiss • Under the Bridge • What It Is • and more.
00699710 . . . .$16.95

Rock 'n' Roll

80 rock 'n' roll classics: At the Hop • Barbara Ann • Chantilly Lace • Crying • Duke of Earl • Great Balls of Fire • I Get Around • It's My Party • La Bamba • Long Tall Sally • The Loco-Motion • My Boyfriend's Back • Peggy Sue • Return to Sender • Rock Around the Clock • Stand by Me • Surfin' U.S.A. • Willie and the Hand Jive • and more.
00699535 . . . .$12.95

Complete contents listings available online at www.halleonard.com